W9-BLY-194

PROFESSOR FIGGY'S

WEATHER & CLIMATE SCIENCE LAB

for KIDS

52 FAMILY-FRIENDLY ACTIVITIES
Exploring Meteorology, Earth Systems, and Climate Change

JIM NOONAN

FOREWORD BY
MARTHA STEWART

QUARRY

Brimming with creative inspiration, how-to projects, and useful information to enrich your everyday life, Quarto Knows is a favorite destination for those pursuing their interests and passions. Visit our site and dig deeper with our books into your area of interest: Quarto Creates, Quarto Cooks, Quarto Homes, Quarto Lives, Quarto Drives, Quarto Explores, Quarto Gifts, or Quarto Kids.

© 2022 Quarto Publishing Group USA Inc.
Text © 2022 Noonan Riegel Projects LLC

First Published in 2022 by Quarry Books, an imprint of The Quarto Group, 100 Cummings Center, Suite 265-D, Beverly, MA 01915, USA.
T (978) 282-9590 F (978) 283-2742 QuartoKnows.com

All rights reserved. No part of this book may be reproduced in any form without written permission of the copyright owners. All images in this book have been reproduced with the knowledge and prior consent of the artists concerned, and no responsibility is accepted by producer, publisher, or printer for any infringement of copyright or otherwise, arising from the contents of this publication. Every effort has been made to ensure that credits accurately comply with information supplied. We apologize for any inaccuracies that may have occurred and will resolve inaccurate or missing information in a subsequent reprinting of the book.

Quarry Books titles are also available at discount for retail, wholesale, promotional, and bulk purchase. For details, contact the Special Sales Manager by email at specialsales@quarto.com or by mail at The Quarto Group, Attn: Special Sales Manager, 100 Cummings Center, Suite 265-D, Beverly, MA 01915, USA.

10 9 8 7 6 5 4 3 2 1

ISBN: 978-0-7603-7085-8

Digital edition published in 2022

eISBN: 978-0-7603-7086-5

Library of Congress Cataloging-in-Publication Data available.

Design, Page Layout, and Illustration: Mattie Wells

Photography: Christina Bohn, except pages 5, 12, 14 (top), 19 (bottom), 30, 34 (bottom), 37 (right), 50, 52, 55 (top), 57, 68, 86, 90 (top), 100 (top), 102 (top), 104, 108 (top), 116 (top), 120 are Shutterstock

Printed in China

Borax, also known by its chemical name sodium tetraborate, is a trademarked product in the United States from Rio Tinto Group. In this book, Borax is used as a material in Lab 2.

PROFESSOR FIGGY'S

WEATHER & CLIMATE SCIENCE LAB
for KIDS

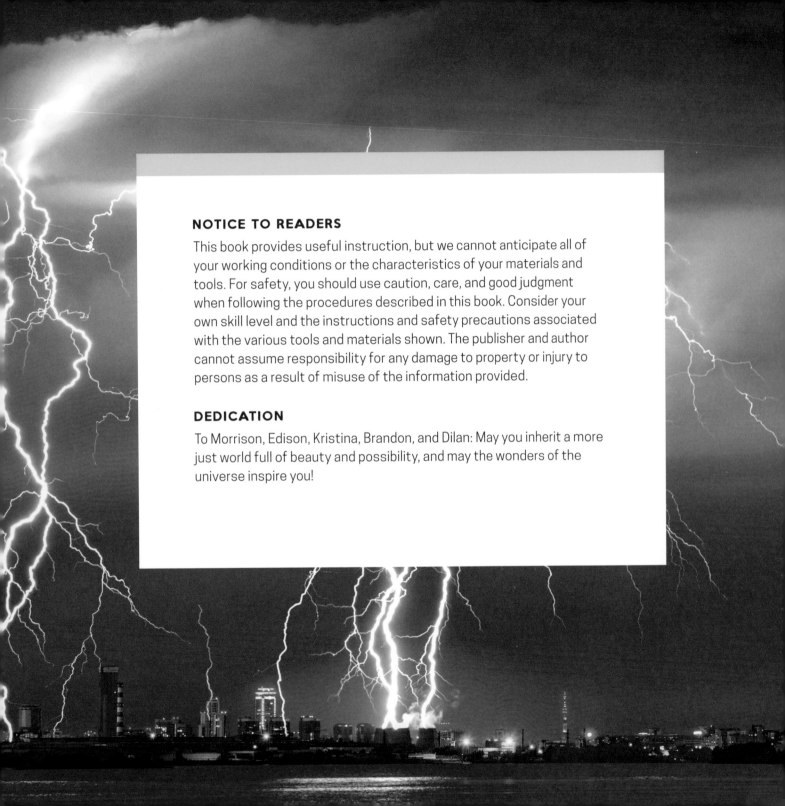

NOTICE TO READERS

This book provides useful instruction, but we cannot anticipate all of your working conditions or the characteristics of your materials and tools. For safety, you should use caution, care, and good judgment when following the procedures described in this book. Consider your own skill level and the instructions and safety precautions associated with the various tools and materials shown. The publisher and author cannot assume responsibility for any damage to property or injury to persons as a result of misuse of the information provided.

DEDICATION

To Morrison, Edison, Kristina, Brandon, and Dilan: May you inherit a more just world full of beauty and possibility, and may the wonders of the universe inspire you!

CONTENTS

UNIT 1
EARTH'S AMAZING ATMOSPHERE

UNIT 2
THE POWER OF THE SUN

UNIT 3
THE CLOUDS & THE RAIN

UNIT 4
THE WINDS THAT BLOW

UNIT 5
SEVERE WEATHER EVENTS

UNIT 6
WHEN IT'S COLD & SNOWY

UNIT 7
CLIMATE IN CRISIS

FOREWORD
By Martha Stewart

It was always exciting, fun, surprising, and educational when Jim Noonan, aka "Professor Figgy," donned his white lab coat and oversized eyeglasses and stepped onto the set of *The Martha Stewart Show*. Each and every episode was a delight, and that we all learned how to make giant crystal snowflakes, glowing fog bubbles, a CD hovercraft powered by balloons, crystal egg geodes, elephant toothpaste, and lava lamps—to name a few—opened our imaginations to infinite possibilities!

It was Professor Figgy's incredible talent as an eccentric educator, with his quirky sense of humor and incredible knowledge of new and old science, that drew us to him. He never ceased to entertain, to teach, to demystify, and to explain in layman's terms the wonders of the universe.

What Figgy, as we called him, did so well was take simple household ingredients, such as school glue and borax, and transform them into something magical and wonderous, like green slime, capturing our imaginations, celebrating creativity, and engendering, in the most friendly way possible, our curiosity!

Jim Noonan has now turned that showmanship, that knowledge of science and nature, that deep curiosity into a magnificent book devoted to understanding weather and climate. And this book is directed at his favorite audience: children of all ages who get a kick out of learning from a wizard, a magician, a true-to-life Merlin.

In fifty-two ingenious projects, Figgy aims to educate and entertain the whole family in the very complex—and at times controversial—science of climate change, weather patterns, and meteorology, encouraging all of us, children

Photos courtesy of Rob Tannenbaum/Watershed Visual Media

Professor Figgy shows Martha the famous Egg-in-a-Bottle experiment. See page 24 to try it!

Figgy jokes with Martha while demonstrating how to make glittery zodiac constellation wall art.

and adults alike, to put on our thinking hats and perhaps strive to make a difference in the frightening world of global warming and climate evolution.

My grandchildren, ages nine and ten, have been fans of Figgy for a long time. This book cements their relationship to his knowledge and teaching skills in a volume designed to please, to entertain, and to inform in an incredibly astute and useful manner.

Thank you, Professor Figgy!

What else do you have up your sleeves???

INTRODUCTION

WEATHER VS. CLIMATE

Weather and climate are not the same thing, but they are related. You have to understand one in order to understand the other, and scientists study and report on both in order to help people live better lives today and in the future.

Weather is the combination of events that occurs in the atmosphere over a short period of time. Changes in temperature, air pressure, humidity, and other factors make the weather cloudy or sunny, windy or calm, or rainy or snowy on any given day. Weather is different in different parts of the world and changes quickly over the course of minutes, hours, days, and weeks.

Climate describes what the weather is like over a longer period of time and in a specific part of the world. There are five basic climate zones: tropical, desert, temperate, continental, and polar. When we talk about climate, we're describing what we would expect the weather to be on a certain day in a certain zone based on lots of weather data gathered over months, years, decades, and even centuries.

WATCHING & MEASURING THE WEATHER

In 350 BCE, Greek philosopher Aristotle wrote a book called *Meteorology*, which comes from the Greek word *meteoron*, meaning "of the atmosphere." Aristotle set out to describe why the weather does what it does, but he was mostly incorrect in his explanations.

It wasn't until the 1600s that scientists started measuring specific factors that affect the weather. Physicists who invented tools to measure air pressure and temperature were some of the first meteorologists. Their early work led to the study and prediction of the weather that's done today with radar and supercomputers.

What you observe when you pay careful attention and use all of your senses gives you very useful data about the weather as it's happening. The activities in this book will ask you to do a lot of observing, measuring, and predicting, sometimes with special tools and sometimes without. By sharpening these skills, these labs will set you on your way to becoming a meteorologist yourself.

OVERVIEW

This book is broken down into seven units with seven to eight activities each, for a total of fifty-two labs for all seasons and all parts of the world. Each unit tackles an important weather or climate topic and lays out labs to investigate specific concepts and questions.

Each lab has a complete list of **Tools & Materials** you'll need, some **Safety Tips, Hints & Tricks** as common-sense guidelines, and a clear and detailed **Protocol**, or list of step-by-step instructions. These are followed by the **Creative Enrichment** section with a bit of "Did You Know?" trivia, follow-up questions for "Taking It Further," or an additional activity called a "Mini Lab." Finally, each lab wraps up with **The Science Behind the Fun**, an easy-to-understand discussion of the observations you made and the questions you asked.

Some of the labs are actual experiments in which you'll build an apparatus or setup. In others, you'll craft colorful models to stand in for things that are too dangerous, too big, or too difficult to see in nature because they only happen in certain places at certain times.

SCIENCE JOURNAL

To make your own science journal, choose a notebook where you can record all of your work in one place and write your name on the front cover.

Before you start each lab, choose the next blank page in your journal and write down the lab's title, the page numbers from the lab book, and the date. Write a quick summary, make a list of the tools and materials you'll use, and jot down any questions you have. Leave plenty of room to record your observations and answer questions along the way.

As you record your data, be detailed and accurate. Always include units with measurement values (abbreviate to save time and space). Feel free to draw diagrams. Don't erase your mistakes—cross them out with a single line to be honest about your process.

When you're finished, write as short or as long a conclusion as you like. How do you feel about the lab? What did you like or dislike? What problems did you encounter? Did you figure out solutions? How can you further explore a concept? What are new ways to investigate the same idea?

UNIT 1
EARTH'S AMAZING ATMOSPHERE

The atmosphere is a remarkable blanket of air that surrounds the Earth. In addition to the oxygen we breathe, it contains gases such as nitrogen and water vapor as well as carbon dioxide and methane. The atmosphere protects us from the dangerous radiation of our sun and the bitter cold of outer space. It is the bubble in which all life on the planet can exist.

There are five layers in the atmosphere. From lowest to highest, they are the troposphere (TROH-poh-sfeer), stratosphere (STRA-toh-sfeer), mesosphere (MEH-soh-sfeer), thermosphere (THER-moh-sfeer), and exosphere (EK-soh-sfeer).

In this unit, you'll begin by crafting a detailed model of the atmosphere's five layers and learning about what happens in each. You'll discover how gas molecules and other particles make the sky look blue and work your way up through the layers, learning about the formation of ozone in the stratosphere, meteors burning up in the mesosphere, and why the northern and southern lights glow in the thermosphere.

You'll finish the unit by building simple devices that demonstrate or measure air pressure, showing how the Earth's gravity keeps the atmosphere in place and how this vast envelope of air pushes down on the Earth's surface with incredible force.

Lab 1

MODEL THE ATMOSPHERE

TOOLS & MATERIALS

- ⊘ craft or construction paper in white, green, yellow, and multiple shades of blue
- ⊘ drawing compass with pencil
- ⊘ ruler
- ⊘ scissors
- ⊘ map of the world (for reference)
- ⊘ glue stick
- ⊘ marker, pen, or pencil
- ⊘ stickers and/or old magazines
- ⊘ craft embellishments, such as glitter, stars, pom-poms, jewels, or beads

SAFETY TIPS, HINTS & TRICKS

- ⊘ A drawing compass has a very sharp point. If you've never used one before, have an adult show you how.
- ⊘ You can also use a series of glasses, plates, bowls, or other round objects to trace paper circles in the suggested sizes.

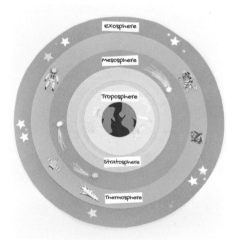

Use simple craft materials to build a two-dimensional model of the Earth's atmosphere.

TIME: 45 MINUTES

Fig. 5: Finish your model with glitter and embellishments.

Fig. 1: Draw and cut out a total of six blue circles, including Earth.

Fig. 2: Make a target with Earth in the middle.

Fig. 3: Cut out and add the ozone layer to your model.

PROTOCOL

STEP 1: Starting with a radius of 1 inch (r = 1", or 2.5 cm) on the compass, draw a circle with a diameter of 2 inches (d = 2", or 5 cm) on a sheet of blue paper and cut it out. Using a world map as a reference, cut out shapes of the continents from green paper and attach them with a glue stick to make Earth.

STEP 2: Draw and cut out five additional circles to create the layers of the atmosphere. (Fig. 1)

Use these measurements:

- r = 2" (5 cm), d = 4" (10 cm): Troposphere
- r = 3" (7.5 cm), d = 6" (15 cm): Stratosphere
- r = 4" (10 cm), d = 8" (20 cm): Mesosphere
- r = 5" (13 cm), d = 10" (25 cm): Thermosphere
- r = 6" (15 cm), d = 12" (30 cm): Exosphere

STEP 3: Use the glue stick to attach the circles one on top of the other, largest to smallest, making what looks like a target. (Fig. 2)

STEP 4: To make the ozone layer, cut a circle with a 5-inch (13 cm) diameter, or 2½-inch (6 cm) radius, out of yellow paper. Then, carefully cut off a strip ¼ inch (6 mm) thick from its circumference to make a thin ring. Use the glue stick to attach this to your model, centered in the stratosphere. (Fig. 3)

CONTINUED

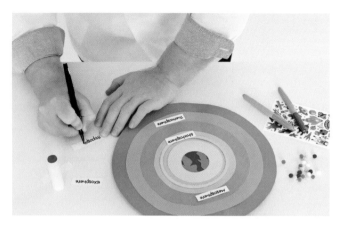

Fig. 4: Add a small, hand-written label to each layer.

STEP 5: Cut five small strips of white paper and write the name of one of the layers of the atmosphere on each. Using the glue stick and Step 2 as a reference, attach these labels to their layers on the model. (Fig. 4)

STEP 6: Using the information in the Science Behind the Fun (at right), flip through your sticker collection or old magazines to find examples of things that exist in each layer. Cut these out and use the glue stick to attach them to their layers.

STEP 7: To complete your model, add glitter for the polar lights and the tails of shooting stars, use colored pompoms as meteorites, and attach jewels and stars in the space of the upper exosphere. (Fig. 5)

CREATIVE ENRICHMENT: TAKING IT FURTHER

- What are the atmospheric "pauses"? (Hint: They're the boundaries between layers, and there are four of them.) Look up their names and label them on your model.

- Do more research on the atmosphere. How far does each layer extend from the surface of the Earth? What is the temperature range and chemical make-up of each? What else can you learn?

THE SCIENCE BEHIND THE FUN

Here's a little bit more information about each of the five layers of the atmosphere to help you with your model.

Troposphere

- This is the "lower" atmosphere, where we live.
- Most clouds and weather happen here.

Stratosphere

- The jet streams flow here.
- Commercial jets fly in its lower portion because there is less turbulence there.

Mesosphere

- Gases here burn up meteors and other space debris.
- Part of the "middle" atmosphere.

Thermosphere

- The northern and southern lights appear here.
- Satellites and the International Space Station orbit here.

Exosphere

- This outermost layer is almost like outer space.
- The air is very thin and gradually "leaks" into space.

AURORA SLIME

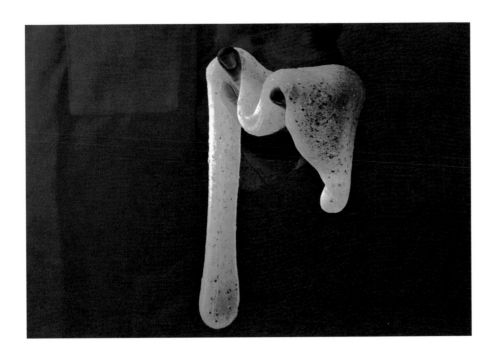

Inspired by the polar lights, this cosmic concoction glows under a black light.

TIME: 45 MINUTES

Fig. 5: Your slime stretches, oozes, and glows!

TOOLS & MATERIALS

- yellow highlighter
- pliers
- 3 bowls or containers
- measuring cup
- hot water
- protective gloves
- measuring spoons
- 4 ounces (½ cup [118 ml]) clear school glue
- 2 teaspoons (5 g) borax laundry booster
- 2 mixing spoons
- 3 types of glitter (fine iridescent, chunky blue, silver and gold stars)
- black light

SAFETY TIPS, HINTS & TRICKS

- Have an adult do the step with pliers—it takes a bit of force to pull apart a highlighter.
- Protect your work surface with newspaper and/or do this lab near the kitchen sink for easy cleanup.

CONTINUED

Fig. 1: Highlighter ink makes the water "glow."

Fig. 2: Make two different solutions for your chemical reaction.

PROTOCOL

STEP 1: Have an adult use a pair of pliers to pry open the bottom of the highlighter and shake out the felt ink cartridge. Then, remove the cap and use the pliers to pull out the felt tip. Place the cartridge and tip in one of the bowls or containers with 2 cups (473 ml) of hot water. Let the mixture sit until the water cools completely. (Fig. 1)

STEP 2: After most of the ink has dissolved in the water, put on gloves and squeeze the felt pieces with your fingers to get out the last drops. Then, discard the felt.

STEP 3: Prepare two separate reaction solutions in two separate bowls or containers:

- Mixture #1 = ⅓ cup (79 ml) highlighter water + 4 ounces (½ cup [118 ml]) glue
- Mixture #2 = ¾ cup (177 ml) highlighter water + 2 teaspoons (5 g) borax

Use a *different spoon* to stir each mixture. Make sure the ingredients are thoroughly blended and dissolved. (Fig. 2)

STEP 4: Pour mixture #2 into mixture #1 while stirring. Try not to get any undissolved borax crystals into the slime. Gather all the slime into the blob that forms and pour off any excess liquid left in the bowl. (Fig. 3)

STEP 5: Add 1 teaspoon each of the different glitters to the bowl. Knead the slime like dough until it becomes smooth and pliable and everything is incorporated. (Fig. 4)

STEP 6: Have fun with your aurora slime! Stretch it slowly or pull it apart quickly. Let it ooze between your fingers. Turn off the lights and turn on a black light to see it glow! (Fig. 5)

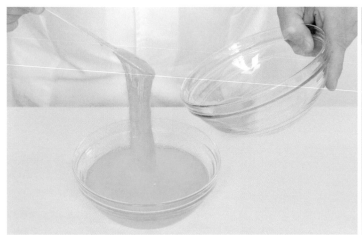

Fig. 3: Mix the two solutions to make a big blob of slime.

Fig. 4: Adding glitter makes your slime shimmer, and kneading makes it smooth and pliable.

CREATIVE ENRICHMENT: SHOOTING STARS MINI LAB

Although you have to be close to the North or South Pole to see the aurora, there are light shows to see in the sky no matter where you are. For example, when a meteor falls through the mesosphere, it burns up at temperatures as high as 3,000°F (1,650°C), giving off a bright streak of light. Spend some time observing the night sky. If you live in a city, try to go somewhere with less light pollution.

- How many shooting stars can you see?
- Where are they located in the sky?
- How long or bright are their tails?
- How many different colors of light can you see?

THE SCIENCE BEHIND THE FUN

The northern lights (*aurora borealis*, uh-ROHR-uh bor-ee-AL-iss) and southern lights (*aurora australis*, uh-ROHR-uh aw-STRALL-iss) occur when the stream of charged particles emitted from the sun (the "solar wind") interacts with the Earth's magnetic field. The solar wind *ionizes* gas particles in the thermosphere (knocks their electrons loose) and creates a state of matter called *plasma* that gives off light in bands of varying color. (Fig. 6)

Fig. 6: The stunning spectacle of the northern lights.

Pyranine, a dye commonly found in yellow highlighter ink, absorbs ultraviolet (UV) rays from black light and emits visible light. No ionization occurs, but just like the gases in the thermosphere, the ink absorbs one kind of radiation and emits another.

WHY IS THE SKY BLUE?

TOOLS & MATERIALS

- ⊘ large, clear glass or plastic rectangular container (approx. 16" L × 8" W × 10" H [41 × 20 × 25 cm])
- ⊘ water
- ⊘ flashlight
- ⊘ white paper
- ⊘ milk
- ⊘ mixing spoon

SAFETY TIPS, HINTS & TRICKS

- ⊘ Do this lab in a room where you can turn off the lights and make it very dark.
- ⊘ The flashlight should emit a strong, focused beam of white light.
- ⊘ If you don't have liquid milk, powdered milk works, too. Be sure it is completely dissolved in the water.
- ⊘ Ask a friend to help so each of you can hold the flashlight while the other observes the light.

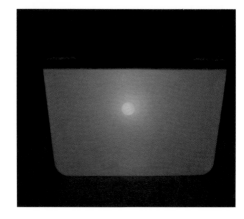

Shining light through a mixture of milk and water shows why the sky is blue and why sunsets are orange and red.

TIME: 15 MINUTES

Fig. 4: Viewed through the short end, the beam looks like the sun at sunset.

PROTOCOL

STEP 1: Fill the container three-quarters full of water and turn off the lights. Shine the flashlight through the container on the long side and onto a sheet of white paper on the other side. What color is the light on the paper? What color is the water?

STEP 2: Now shine the flashlight into the short side of the container. What do you observe through the long side? What does the beam look like when viewed through the short end? (Fig. 1)

STEP 3: Turn on the lights. Add 1 to 2 tablespoons (15 to 30 ml) of milk to the water and stir with the mixing spoon until the water is slightly cloudy. (Fig. 2)

STEP 4: Turn off the lights and shine the flashlight into the short side of the container. What color is the liquid? What color is the light beam when viewed through the long side? Does it change over the length of the container? (Fig. 3)

Fig. 1: Shine your flashlight through the container filled with just water.

Fig. 2: The milk and water mixed together simulate the sky.

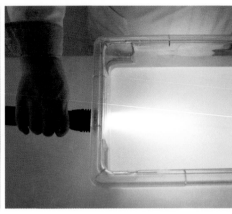

Fig. 3: Closest to the flashlight, the beam appears blue.

STEP 5: If you hold up a piece of white paper, what color is the light emerging from the container? What does the beam look like now when viewed through the short end of the container? (Fig. 4)

CREATIVE ENRICHMENT: POLARIZATION MINI LAB

1. Look at your setup through a pair of polarized sunglasses. How is the beam's appearance different with the glasses on?

2. Place one lens of the glasses between the flashlight and the container. Turn the lens while a partner views the beam from the top and you view it from the side. What do you observe?

THE SCIENCE BEHIND THE FUN

Visible light contains waves of different wavelengths. Violet and blue wavelengths are shorter while orange and red wavelengths are longer. Sunlight contains all colors, but not in an equal mix—it's made up of more orange-red light and contains a greater amount of blue light than violet light.

When the sun's rays collide with gas molecules in the atmosphere, they scatter in many different directions. Shorter wavelengths scatter the most. Because there is more blue light than violet in sunlight, and because our eyes are more sensitive to the color, the sky appears blue.

When you view the sun rising or setting, it is farther away from you than when it is overhead and the light rays have to travel a longer distance through more atmosphere to get to your eyes. This scatters the shorter wavelengths and leaves a higher concentration of yellow, orange, and red. The same thing applies to milk proteins dissolved in water.

Wearing polarized sunglasses filters out any light not vibrating in the vertical plane of the lenses. This makes the beam appear sharper and brighter. Placing a lens in front of the flashlight polarizes the beam itself. When it's vertically polarized, the side viewer sees a bright beam and the viewer above sees a dim beam. When the lens is turned 90 degrees, the reverse occurs.

MODEL OZONE FORMATION

TOOLS & MATERIALS:

- ⌾ toothpicks
- ⌾ gumdrops, gummy bears, or other soft candy

SAFETY TIPS, HINTS & TRICKS

- ⌾ Choose two different colors of candy to act as oxygen and nitrogen atoms.
- ⌾ The toothpicks model molecular bonds and represent a pair of electrons shared between atoms.

Fig. 1: Make a bunch of oxygen (O_2) molecules. Connect the atoms with double bonds.

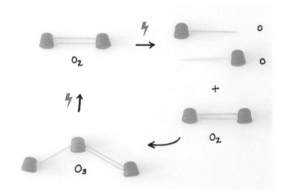

Use candy and toothpicks to model the formation of ozone in the stratosphere and near the ground.

TIME: 30 MINUTES

Fig. 2: A candy model of the oxygen/ozone cycle

PROTOCOL

STEP 1: Build oxygen molecules as they are found in the atmosphere. You'll need two oxygen atoms and two toothpicks for each one. (Fig. 1)

STEP 2: Model how ozone is formed in the stratosphere. Act like UV light and split some of your O_2 molecules into two pieces of candy, each with a toothpick sticking out of it. Then, combine one of these with an intact O_2 molecule to form a molecule of ozone (O_3). (Fig. 2)

STEP 3: Make nitrogen dioxide (NO_2) molecules, which are found in the waste gases of burning fossil fuels. You'll need two oxygen atoms, one nitrogen atom, and three toothpicks. (Fig. 3)

STEP 4: Now, model how ozone is formed much closer to the ground. Act like UV light and split a single oxygen atom with one toothpick off of the nitrogen dioxide, leaving behind double-bonded nitric oxide (NO).

STEP 5: As in Step 2, combine a single oxygen atom with a whole oxygen molecule to form a molecule of ozone. (Fig. 4)

Fig. 3: Connect two oxygens to one nitrogen at an angle as shown.

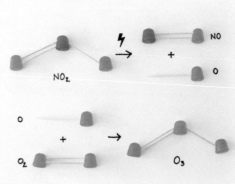

Fig. 4: Split an oxygen atom (O) off of NO_2 and combine it with oxygen (O_2) to form ozone (O_3).

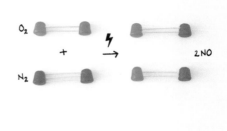

Fig. 5: Lightning splits nitrogen and oxygen molecules in the air into single atoms that recombine as nitric oxide.

STEP 6: Make nitrogen (N_2) molecules as they're found in the atmosphere. You'll need two nitrogen atoms and three toothpicks for each one.

STEP 7: Break apart a nitrogen molecule and an oxygen molecule and reconfigure them into nitric oxide to model one way that the heat of a lightning bolt can influence the formation of ozone. (Fig. 5)

STEP 8: React two molecules of nitric oxide with another molecule of oxygen to form two molecules of nitrogen dioxide.

STEP 9: Finally, act like UV radiation again and split the nitrogen dioxide back into nitric oxide and a free oxygen atom that can now combine with an oxygen molecule to form ozone.

CREATIVE ENRICHMENT: DID YOU KNOW?

In the 1980s, scientists discovered that humanmade chemicals called chlorofluorocarbons (CFCs) were causing a thinning, or "hole," in the ozone layer. When exposed to UV light, these CFCs release energized chlorine (Cl) atoms, which destroy ozone.

This discovery led to the Montreal Protocol of 1987, which banned many ozone-depleting substances. The hole is slowly recovering, and scientists project that ozone will return to pre-1980 levels between 2050 and 2070.

THE SCIENCE BEHIND THE FUN

In the stratosphere, UV rays from the sun split oxygen molecules into separate oxygen atoms in a process called photolysis (fo-TALL-uh-sis). These oxygen atoms quickly react with nearby oxygen molecules to make ozone.

More UV rays then break off ozone's third oxygen atom, which quickly reacts with another oxygen molecule to form ozone again in a process called interconversion. This continuous action generates heat, which gives the stratosphere unique temperature properties.

EGG IN A BOTTLE

TOOLS & MATERIALS

- ⊘ glass milk bottle or similar container with an opening slightly smaller than the diameter of your egg
- ⊘ vegetable oil
- ⊘ newspaper, torn into small pieces
- ⊘ matches or lighter
- ⊘ hard-boiled egg, peeled

SAFETY TIPS, HINTS & TRICKS

- ⊘ This experiment involves fire. Only adults should handle matches or a lighter.
- ⊘ Set up your apparatus in an area with good ventilation and have a way to extinguish the fire, if necessary.

Take a trip to the kitchen for a fun and easy lesson in the power of air pressure.

TIME: 15 MINUTES

Fig. 3: Differences in air pressure force the egg into the bottle.

PROTOCOL

STEP 1: With your finger, apply a small amount of vegetable oil to the top and inside rim of the bottle's opening. (Fig. 1)

STEP 2: Have an adult ignite a small piece of newspaper with the matches or lighter and drop it inside the bottle. (Fig. 2)

STEP 3: Immediately place the egg on the mouth of the bottle with the pointier end facing downward. Pay close attention. Do you notice anything happening between the mouth of the bottle and the egg? What happens when the flame goes out, and why? (Fig. 3)

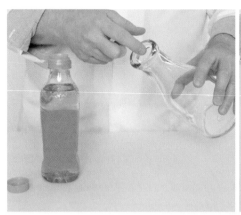

Fig. 1: Use the oil to provide a bit of lubrication for the egg.

Fig. 2: Use extra caution when lighting the newspaper.

Fig. 4: Use a straw and your breath to pop the egg out of the bottle.

CREATIVE ENRICHMENT: TAKING IT FURTHER

How would you reverse the experiment and get the egg out of the bottle?

HINT: Flatten a straw with your fingers. Put it in the bottle's mouth and turn it up at an angle. Wedge the straw between the egg and the inside of the bottle, creating a seal. Blow air through the straw with enough force to push the egg out. Extra points if you can keep it whole! (Fig. 4)

THE SCIENCE BEHIND THE FUN

The Earth's immense gravitational pull keeps the atmosphere in place. All of that air is heavy, and it pushes down on everything on the surface with a force of almost 15 pounds per square inch, also known as 1 atmosphere (1 atm) of air pressure. We can't feel this pressure though, because the air pushes on everything equally and in every direction.

When you drop a piece of lit newspaper into the bottle and cap it with the egg, the air in the bottle heats up, making it expand, which in turn increases its pressure. The air pushes its way out, making the egg jump on the opening.

When the flame consumes all the oxygen or all the paper, it goes out. The air inside cools and contracts while the egg seals the mouth, which lowers the pressure inside and creates a small vacuum. The higher (atmospheric) pressure outside pushes on the egg and forces it into the bottle.

THE CARTESIAN DIVER

TOOLS & MATERIALS

- clear plastic soda bottle, empty and clean
- warm, soapy water or adhesive remover
- funnel
- water
- glass eyedropper
- drinking glass

Investigate pressure and buoyancy inside a simple toy made from a soda bottle.

TIME: 15 MINUTES

Fig. 4: Squeeze the bottle to make the dropper dive.

SAFETY TIPS, HINTS & TRICKS

- 1-liter plastic bottles work well for this lab, but use whatever bottle you have on hand—it can be smaller or larger.

PROTOCOL

STEP 1: Soak the bottle in warm, soapy water or use adhesive remover to get off any labels and sticky residue. Wash and rinse the bottle thoroughly. Fill it to the top with water using the funnel. (Fig. 1)

STEP 2: Fill the drinking glass three-quarters full of water. Squeeze the bulb to fill the dropper with enough water so that it just floats upright in the glass. This is the "diver." (Fig. 2)

STEP 3: Place the diver in the neck of the bottle. Some water will spill out, which is okay as long as the bottle remains completely full. Screw the cap on tightly. (Fig. 3)

Fig. 1: Clean your 1-liter bottle and fill it with water.

Fig. 2: The diver should just float in the water.

Fig. 3: Put in the diver and screw on the cap.

STEP 4: Squeeze the sides of the bottle firmly between your thumb and fingers. What happens to the diver? Release the sides of the bottle. What happens now? Can you squeeze the bottle just enough to float the diver in the middle of the column of water? (Fig. 4)

CREATIVE ENRICHMENT: TAKING IT FURTHER

Replace the diver with a packet of ketchup, mustard, or soy sauce. (Make sure it actually floats first.) How is the packet different from the original diver? Does the same thing happen? Why or why not?

THE SCIENCE BEHIND THE FUN

The "Cartesian" (kar-TEE-zhen) Diver is an example of Archimedes's (ar-kuh-MEE-deez) principle—the physical law of buoyancy (BOY-uhn-see), which says the upward force on an object submerged in a fluid is equal to the weight of the fluid the object displaces.

The force of your fingers on the bottle squeezes the air bubble inside the diver's bulb into a smaller space. Water flows in to balance the volume change, which makes the diver weigh more than the water it displaces, and it sinks. When you release the pressure, the air expands and pushes water out of the dropper. This makes the diver more buoyant, and it floats upward.

When a condiment packet is sealed during manufacturing, a small bubble of air can get trapped inside. Squeezing the bottle compresses the air bubble. This makes the packet smaller, which means it displaces less water. The packet sinks because its weight is now greater than the weight of the water it displaces.

BUILD A BAROMETER

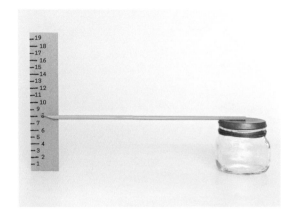

Make a simple tool to measure atmospheric pressure and forecast the weather using a jar, a balloon, and drinking straws.

TIME: 30 MINUTES

Fig. 5: The pointer moves up and down the gauge as the air pressure and weather change.

TOOLS & MATERIALS

- latex balloon
- scissors
- glass jar
- rubber bands
- 2 plastic drinking straws
- heavy-duty, fast-drying glue
- tape
- small piece of cardstock or thin cardboard
- ruler
- marker, pen, or pencil

SAFETY TIPS, HINTS & TRICKS

- Be sure to use a balloon that has never been blown up before, so the latex is taut.
- When you stretch the balloon, have a friend or parent help make it as secure as possible.

PROTOCOL

STEP 1: Cut off the neck of the balloon with the scissors.

STEP 2: Stretch the remaining round part of the balloon over the mouth of the jar and secure it with two rubber bands. (Fig. 1)

STEP 3: Cut both ends of one straw at an angle to create points. Insert one of the cut ends into one end of the second straw. (Fig. 2)

STEP 4: Attach the non-pointy end of the combined straw pointer to the center of the balloon with glue. Be sure the pointer is straight and at a right angle to the jar. Hold it in place with a piece of tape until the glue sets. (Fig. 3)

Fig. 1: Seal the jar well with a tightly stretched balloon and rubber bands.

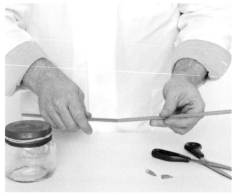
Fig. 2: Make a long, straight pointer with two straws.

Fig. 3: Attach the long, straight pointer to your barometer.

Fig. 4: Use a ruler as a gauge or mark out your own.

STEP 5: With a ruler, a marker, and a piece of cardstock, make a gauge with equally spaced marks every ½ inch (or 1 cm) apart. Number each mark, starting from the bottom. (Fig. 4)

STEP 6: Attach the gauge to a vertical surface and position your barometer so it is pointing at it. Over several days, record the markings indicated by the pointer. Take readings every few hours and compare the values. Are they increasing or decreasing? Also note the weather each time you take a reading. How does it change? (Fig. 5)

CREATIVE ENRICHMENT: DID YOU KNOW?

In 1643, Italian physicist Evangelista Torricelli made the very first barometer by taking a long glass tube sealed at one end and filling it with mercury. Careful not to let any air in, he tipped it upside down and stood it in a bowl of mercury. A vacuum formed above the liquid metal, and Torricelli observed that the mercury's height in the tube varied from day to day.

THE SCIENCE BEHIND THE FUN

Atmospheric pressure varies around the planet as the sun unevenly warms the Earth's surface, causing air masses to rise and fall. Warm, rising air creates areas of low pressure while cool, falling air creates high pressure.

When you sealed off the jar with the balloon, you captured a volume of air inside. The outside air pressure and the pressure inside the jar were equal. But as the weather changes, so does the air pressure.

The higher atmospheric pressure of nice weather pushes down on the balloon and the straw's glued end. The edge of the jar acts as a pivot point, and the straw's other end moves up. The opposite happens as storms approach. Because of higher pressure inside the jar, the balloon and the glued end of the straw go up while the pointer goes down.

UNIT 2
THE POWER OF THE SUN

To ancient Egyptians, the sun was the god Ra, the bringer of light and life and ruler of the skies, earth, and underworld. The sun moved as Ra rode his chariot across the sky each day. In the evening, he died as the sun set and descended into the underworld. Each morning with the sunrise, he was reborn.

Thousands of years later, we know the sun is a star powered by nuclear fusion that releases energy as electromagnetic radiation. Traveling outward into space at the speed of light (186,287 mph [299.792 km/s]) and reaching the Earth in 8.3 minutes, this energy warms the planet's surface and fuels the weather in our atmosphere.

In this unit, you'll explore the amazing properties and incredible power of the sun's energy. You'll play with colors of visible light in a "magic light box" and carefully construct a device to tell time with the sun. With fun and easy-to-build setups, you'll harness solar energy to make s'mores, spin pinwheels, brew tea, and purify water.

You'll finish out the unit making beautiful sun prints with leaves and construction paper, and you'll learn how plants capture sunlight to drive photosynthesis, making food from carbon dioxide and water and releasing oxygen into the air.

MAGIC LIGHT BOX

Explore light color and pigment with this unique toy made from recycled and household materials.

TIME: 1½ HOURS

Fig. 5: Experiment with different combinations of colored water bottles.

TOOLS & MATERIALS

- large cardboard box (approximately 24" x 24" x 36" [61 x 61 x 91 cm])
- white paper
- cellophane tape or glue stick
- packing tape
- ruler or measuring tape
- pencil, pen, or marker
- utility or craft knife
- drawing compass
- 6 identical 16-ounce (473 ml) plastic bottles, empty and clean
- water
- liquid food coloring (red, blue, green, and yellow)
- aluminum foil
- 2 opaque plastic cups or containers

SAFETY TIPS, HINTS & TRICKS

- If you don't have a drawing compass, you can use a round object, such as a drinking glass or a small bowl.
- This lab involves cutting cardboard with a sharp knife—this should be done by an adult.
- Larger bottles can be used if that's all you have on hand.
- The opaque plastic cups or containers should fit over your bottles.

Fig. 1: Open and flatten the box. Line the inside with white paper.

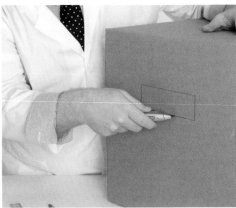
Fig. 2: Be sure to cut cleanly through the cardboard and paper lining.

Fig. 3: The circles should be identical and slightly smaller than the bottles' diameters.

PROTOCOL

STEP 1: Carefully take the box apart and lay it flat. Using the tape or glue stick, line the entire inside surface with white paper, overlapping as needed. (Fig. 1)

STEP 2: Reassemble the box and secure the flaps with the packing tape. Turn the box so the flap sides face to the left and right and the smooth sides face up, down, front, and back.

STEP 3: With a ruler and pencil, draw a 6-inch-wide by 2-inch-tall (15 x 5 cm) rectangle on the front side of the box. Have an adult cut it out with the utility or craft knife to create a viewing slot. (Fig. 2)

STEP 4: Measure the diameter of your bottles. Draw or trace two slightly smaller, identical circles, equally spaced, in the center of the top of the box. Have an adult cut out the circles. (Fig. 3)

CONTINUED

CREATIVE ENRICHMENT: TAKING IT FURTHER

Insert a pair of water bottles of the same color into the box. Place an object that is the same color as one of the bottles inside the box. Observe and record what color the object appears under which color light. Try a red apple with green water bottles. What do you see? What color does a yellow banana appear to be under blue light? What about a green shirt under red light?

Fig. 4: Cover the top with foil with the shiny side out.

STEP 5: To focus more light into the bottles, cover the top of the box with aluminum foil with the shiny side facing out. Secure the foil with glue or tape. Be sure to cut open the circular holes. (Fig. 4)

STEP 6: Fill the bottles with water. Leave two of them clear and add 15 drops of a different food coloring (red, blue, yellow, or green) to each of the remaining four. Cap all the bottles, and shake to mix.

STEP 7: Take your box outside on a sunny day and insert both bottles of clear water (bottom first) into the holes. Look through the viewing slot and describe what patterns and colors you see.

STEP 8: Experiment with the colored water bottles. Keep a record of different combinations and describe what you see with each. Cover one bottle with an opaque cup or container. What changes in the light do you observe? (Fig. 5)

THE SCIENCE BEHIND THE FUN

The primary light colors are red, blue, and green. When mixed in pairs, primary colors produce secondary light colors: red + blue = magenta, blue + green = cyan, and red + green = yellow. When all the primary or all the secondary colors are mixed, or when a primary is mixed with its complementary secondary color, the resulting light is white. (Fig. 6)

The opposite is true for pigments. The primary colors of pigments are cyan, magenta, and yellow. True black is the presence of all pigment colors, while white is the absence of any. (Fig. 7)

Pigments work by reflecting a particular color of light back to your eye while absorbing all others. When an object is exposed only to wavelengths that it absorbs, there is no light for it to reflect, and it appears black—like a red apple under green light, a yellow banana under blue light, or a green shirt under red light.

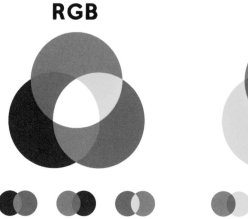

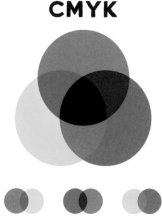

Fig. 6: RGB and the "additive" properties of light.

Fig. 7: CMYK and the "subtractive" properties of pigments.

COOK WITH THE SUN

Cook your favorite treats in a solar oven constructed from a simple cardboard box and aluminum foil.

TIME: 2½ HOURS

Fig. 5: Carefully remove the lid of the oven and place the pie pan inside.

TOOLS & MATERIALS

- medium-sized cardboard box, preferably with a lid
- ruler or straightedge
- utility knife or box cutter
- aluminum foil
- black paper
- scissors
- glue stick
- clear plastic wrap
- tape
- stick, skewer, or pencil
- dark stones
- oven thermometer (analog)
- oven mitts or potholders
- aluminum pie pans
- s'mores components: graham crackers, chocolate bars, and marshmallows

SAFETY TIPS, HINTS, & TRICKS

- To do this lab, you'll need a hot, sunny day with temperatures at or above 80°F (27°C) and not much wind.
- Your box should be at least 3 inches (7.5 cm) deep and big enough to fit the pie pan.
- This oven actually gets hot! Please use care when handling any of its components.
- Because of the heat and the use of cutting tools, an adult should be present to supervise and help as needed.

CONTINUED

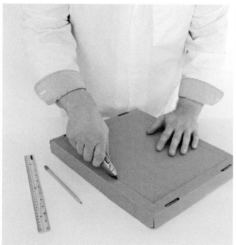

Fig. 1: Make a flap in the box's lid.

Fig. 2: Line your oven with foil and black paper.

Fig. 3: Reflect as much direct sunlight as possible into the box to pre-heat the oven.

PROTOCOL

STEP 1: Using the ruler and utility knife or box cutter, cut a three-sided flap into the lid of the box. Leave a 1-inch (2.5 cm) margin around the sides. Bend the flap upward. (Fig. 1)

STEP 2: Line the flap and the insides of the lid and box with aluminum foil with the shiny side facing outward. Line the inside bottom with black paper. Trim the foil and paper with scissors as needed and secure everything with a glue stick. Make sure all the surfaces are smooth. (Fig. 2)

STEP 3: Layer two pieces of plastic wrap together and tape them on the underside of the lid across the cut opening. Make sure it is pulled taut and sealed well.

STEP 4: Place five or six dark stones and the oven thermometer in the bottom of the oven.

STEP 5: Put the lid on the oven, place it in full and direct sunlight, and prop open the reflective flap with the stick or other rigid object. Let the solar oven sit in the sun for at least 30 minutes and observe the temperature as it preheats. How long does it take to get to its hottest? (Fig. 3)

STEP 6: Prep your s'mores materials in the pie pan, layering a square of graham cracker, a marshmallow or two, a square of chocolate, and a final square of graham cracker. (Fig. 4)

STEP 7: Carefully remove the lid of the oven, place the pie pan on the rocks, and re-cover the oven immediately. Keep an eye on your s'mores and the temperature inside the oven. (Fig. 5)

STEP 8: After about 45 minutes, the marshmallow should be warm and squishy and the chocolate melted. You can now carefully remove the pie pan and enjoy a delicious, solar-cooked treat! (Fig. 6)

Fig. 4: Put the chocolate on top of the marshmallow so everything melts together nicely.

Fig. 6: A sweet reward for all your hard work!

CREATIVE ENRICHMENT: TAKING IT FURTHER

1. Fill silicone molds with broken bits of crayons and put them in your oven for 45 minutes. The bits will melt together into multicolored shapes. Let them cool for an hour before you use them.

2. How can you make your oven more efficient? Try changing its size or shape or use different materials to line the box. A reflective car windshield screen, for example, is shinier and more insulating than foil.

THE SCIENCE BEHIND THE FUN

Solar ovens are designed to absorb and hold heat from the sun. Sunlight hits the reflective flap and is directed into the box. The black paper and dark stones absorb this light and convert it into heat.

The plastic wrap in the lid acts like the roof of a greenhouse and holds the heat in, while the foil and cardboard provide insulation. The stones heat up slowly but hold the heat longer than air, cardboard, paper, or foil, keeping temperatures stable for extended heating times.

In ideal conditions, your oven can reach temperatures of 160°F to 200°F (71°C to 93°C). On a hot, sunny afternoon at 80°F (27°C) or above, it takes about 30 to 60 minutes in a preheated oven for marshmallows to become soft and chocolate to melt.

SOLAR CLOCK

With a plate and a straw, you can build a simple tool that uses the sun to tell time.

TIME: 1 DAY

Fig. 4: Test your sundial's accuracy. How well does it tell the time?

TOOLS & MATERIALS

- paper or plastic plate
- drinking straw
- small ball of clay
- glue or tape
- protractor
- rock or paperweight
- navigational compass
- watch or clock (with a timer and alarm)
- permanent felt-tip marker
- ruler

SAFETY TIPS, HINTS & TRICKS

- Do this lab outside on a clear, sunny day. Give yourself the whole day—start early in the morning once the sun comes up and go until sunset.
- Instead of a drinking straw, you can use a bamboo skewer, a pencil, a stick, or anything else long and straight.
- Have an adult show you how to find north or south with a compass—it takes some practice.
- Be sure never to look directly at the sun when using your sundial!

PROTOCOL

STEP 1: Flip the plate over so that the bottom faces up. Attach the small ball of clay to the center of the plate with some glue or a piece of tape. Insert the straw into the ball of clay at a 75 to 80 degree angle to act as a *gnomon* (NOH-min). (Fig. 1)

STEP 2: Bring the sundial outside and place it in the sun on a flat, level surface, away from any shadows. If you live in the Northern Hemisphere, point the gnomon to the north; if you live in the Southern Hemisphere, point it to the south. Use the compass to determine the direction.

STEP 3: Place the rock or paperweight on the plate, opposite the angle of the gnomon, to hold it down.

STEP 4: Every hour, on the hour, observe the shadow of the gnomon—set a timer and an alarm so you don't forget. Use a marker and a ruler to draw a line, tracing where the shadow falls. Label the line with the time. (Fig. 2)

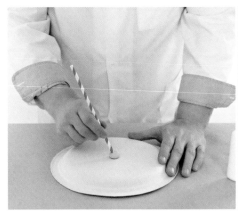

Fig. 1: A gnomon is the piece of a sundial that shows the time with its shadow.

Fig. 2: Observe the shadow every hour and trace a line.

Fig. 3: The lines should look like the spokes of a bicycle wheel.

STEP 5: Once you've recorded shadow lines and times for the entire day, take your sundial inside. (Fig. 3)

STEP 6: The next day, take your sundial back outside and place it in the same exact spot with the gnomon pointing in the same direction as before. Observe the shadow of the gnomon over the course of the day and compare its reading to the actual time. How accurate is your sundial? (Fig. 4)

CREATIVE ENRICHMENT: LIFE-SIZE SUNDIAL MINI LAB

Grab some sidewalk chalk and a friend and find a wide-open, flat concrete or asphalt surface, such as a driveway, playground, or sports court. (For safety's sake, please don't do this in the street or on the sidewalk.) Stand in the center and trace around your shoes. Have your friend trace your shadow. After an hour goes by, stand in the same spot and have your friend trace your shadow again. Do this at least three times. What do you observe about your shadow?

THE SCIENCE BEHIND THE FUN

At any point during the day, the sun's light shines on only half of the Earth's surface. When you see the sun rising in the east, your part of the world is on the very edge of the sunlit portion of the planet, and objects (such as gnomons) cast shadows toward the west.

As the Earth rotates in a counter-clockwise direction, the shadow on the sundial moves clockwise. At noon, the sun is at its highest point in the sky. If shadows are cast at all, they point to the north. As the sun moves toward setting in the west, the gnomon's shadow continues moving toward the east.

Lab 11

BUILD A SOLAR CHIMNEY

TOOLS & MATERIALS

- ⊙ 3 large tin cans
- ⊙ safety can opener
- ⊙ tape (electrical tape, if possible)
- ⊙ large paper clip or piece of rigid wire
- ⊙ pushpin, thumbtack, or straight pin
- ⊙ printer or notebook paper, cut to 6" x 6" (15 × 15 cm)
- ⊙ ruler
- ⊙ scissors
- ⊙ glue stick or cellophane tape
- ⊙ 2 books of the same thickness, about 1½" to 2" (3.5 to 5 cm)

SAFETY TIPS, HINTS & TRICKS

- ⊙ Coffee cans or large bean cans work well for the column.
- ⊙ Because of its flexibility and stickiness, electrical tape works best in this lab, but you can use any tape you have on hand.
- ⊙ If you don't have a safety can opener, cover the cut edges of the cans with tape.

Make a solar updraft tower from recycled cans and tape.

TIME: 45 MINUTES

Fig. 5: Your solar chimney is working when the pinwheel spins.

PROTOCOL

STEP 1: Use the can opener to remove both the top and bottom lids from each can. Clean and dry each can, then tape them together to create a long cylinder. (Fig. 1)

STEP 2: Bend the paper clip or wire into an arch. Tape it across the top of the can column.

STEP 3: Tape the pushpin in the center of the arch, facing upward. (Fig. 2)

Fig. 1: Make a column with cans and tape.

STEP 4: Make a pinwheel out of the piece of paper. Fold the square along both diagonals, cut a 3-inch (7.5 cm) slit into each corner along the fold, and bend the right side of each corner into the center without pressing or flattening the fold. Secure the points with cellophane tape or a glue stick. (Fig. 3)

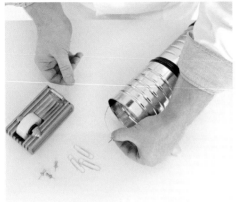

Fig. 2: Make a pointy arch with a paper clip and a pushpin. Tape everything in place.

Fig. 3: How to make a pinwheel.

Fig. 4: Set up your tower and carefully balance the pinwheel.

STEP 5: Place the books on a sunny surface with a 2-inch (5 cm) gap between them. Place the can column on the books with the bottom opening over the gap. Balance the pinwheel, taped or glued side down, on the point of the pushpin. (Fig. 4)

STEP 6: Observe the pinwheel after about 15 to 20 minutes. What do you notice? Why does this happen? What's happening inside the tower? (Fig. 5)

CREATIVE ENRICHMENT: TAKING IT FURTHER

1. What happens if you place the tower directly on the surface, without the books? Does the pinwheel spin?

2. Try painting your tower with flat black craft paint. What effect does this have, and why?

3. What happens if you change the size of the pinwheel? How does the temperature or amount of sun affect the pinwheel's speed?

THE SCIENCE BEHIND THE FUN

In energy-efficient buildings, solar chimneys are used for "passive" heating and cooling. Having no moving parts, they depend entirely on the energy of the sun to work.

Just like your tower, they're often constructed of black and/or metal materials that absorb sunlight and conduct heat, which guarantees a maximum amount of energy being transferred to the column of air inside.

If the top vent of a solar chimney is closed, warmed air is forced into the living space as cooler air is pulled from the room back into the chimney to be heated. To cool a space, the vent is kept open so that heated air can flow up and out, pulling in cool, fresh air through a vent on the other side of the building.

Similarly, the sun heats your tower and the air inside, causing that air to expand, become less dense, and rise out the top of the column. This spins the pinwheel. The space between the two books allows more air to be pulled in at the bottom, keeping the updraft going.

MAKE SUN TEA

Lab 12

TOOLS & MATERIALS

- large glass container with a tight-fitting lid
- water, bottled or distilled
- black tea, bags or loose
- sweetener (optional)
- sliced citrus fruit, such as lemon, lime, or orange (optional)

Make a classic summertime drink without ever turning on the stove.

TIME: 4 HOURS

Fig. 3: Always add sweetener and garnishes *after* steeping the tea and cool it right away.

SAFETY TIPS, HINTS & TRICKS

- Sun tea must be refrigerated immediately after it's made. Consume it on the day you brew it and throw out any leftovers.
- If your tea is thick or syrupy, or if it has a bad odor, do not drink it.
- You can sweeten your tea (*after* brewing) with simple syrup, agave, honey, stevia, or any other sweetener.
- If you plan to garnish your tea, have an adult slice up the citrus with a sharp knife.

PROTOCOL

STEP 1: With warm, soapy water, thoroughly wash your glass container. This can be a beverage dispenser with a spigot or a very large jar or jug with a lid that fits tightly and securely.

STEP 2: For every gallon of water, use 6 to 8 tea bags (or 6 to 8 tablespoons [12 to 18 g] loose tea). Standard black tea or any other caffeinated tea is recommended since caffeine can be a first line of defense against bacteria.

STEP 3: Add your tea to the container and pour in room-temperature bottled or distilled water. Avoid using tap or well water, which can contain unwanted microbes. (Fig. 1)

STEP 4: Place the lid securely on the container and set it in the sun. Steep for at least 2 hours but not more than 4. Set a timer if necessary. If it's a very sunny, hot day, the tea can take less time. (Fig. 2)

STEP 5: Once the tea has fully steeped, remove the tea bags or strain out the loose tea. Sweeten and add citrus slices if you want. Add ice or refrigerate immediately. (Fig. 3)

Fig. 1: Mix the tea and water in a very clean large glass container.

Fig. 2: How long the mixture sits in the sun determines how strong the final tea will be.

STEP 6: Enjoy your sun tea! While sipping your refreshment, think about the following questions: What forces are at play in this lab? Why does making tea with the sun work?

CREATIVE ENRICHMENT: TAKING IT FURTHER

1. Brew some tea with boiling water and perform a taste test with your sun tea. What's the difference in the flavor and color of each?

2. Try the same setup with coffee and do a similar taste test. What else can you brew with the sun?

THE SCIENCE BEHIND THE FUN

When brewing like this, the heat that would usually come from a stovetop is replaced by the sun's energy. Because of variations in the container and the starting water temperature, the mixture is heated unevenly. This causes swirling (convection) currents that steep and naturally mix the tea, so over time, the concentration becomes even throughout. Organic compounds in the tea called *tannins* lend their golden-brown color to the water and give the tea a noticeable "dry" flavor.

The United States Centers for Disease Control and Prevention (CDC) recommend not making sun tea because of possible growth of the bacteria *Alcaligenes viscolactis* (al-KA-luh-jeenz vis-koh-LAK-tuhs). Named for the thickening, or "ropiness," it causes in milk, this microbe can make you sick. That said, if you follow all this lab's safety tips and instructions, you should be okay.

SOLAR WATER PURIFIER

TOOLS & MATERIALS

- large bowl
- small bowl
- measuring cup
- water
- measuring spoons
- table salt
- mixing spoon
- plastic wrap
- tape
- small stone

SAFETY TIPS, HINTS & TRICKS

- A few additional items you'll need for this lab are time, patience, and sunlight.
- You'll be tasting the water to confirm the purification process, so be sure all your tools and materials are very clean and food safe.

Harness the energy of the sun to remove impurities from water.

TIME: 1 TO 2 DAYS

Fig. 3: Beads of condensation show that the solar purifier is working.

PROTOCOL

STEP 1: Measure 2 cups (473 ml) of water and pour it into the large bowl. Add 1 tablespoon (18 g) of table salt and stir with the mixing spoon until completely dissolved. Taste the water—it should be very salty.

STEP 2: Place a small bowl in the center of the large bowl. Be sure that the edge of the inside bowl is lower than the edge of the outside bowl and that the salty water doesn't get into the small bowl. (Fig. 1)

STEP 3: Cover the bowls loosely with plastic wrap and secure it with tape.

STEP 4: Place the stone in the center of the plastic wrap to create a dip in it. Be sure the edge of the small bowl is not touching the plastic. (Fig. 2)

STEP 5: Place your setup in a sunny spot indoors. Let it work for at least a few hours and up to a day or two. What do you observe over time? Do you notice condensation forming on the plastic wrap? (Fig. 3)

Fig. 1: A small bowl nested in a large bowl with the salty water.

Fig. 2: The plastic wrap should be a little loose so the stone can make it dip.

STEP 6: Remove the plastic wrap and observe how much water has gathered in the small bowl. How does this water taste compared to the water in the large bowl?

TIP: If you don't want to taste the purified water, you can evaporate it quickly using a microwave or a pan on the stove to see if it leaves behind any salt.

CREATIVE ENRICHMENT: TAKING IT FURTHER

1. What other liquids or solutions can you try this with? Do the substances dissolved in the water affect whether or not it can be purified?

2. Try adding food coloring to the water. Does this affect the color of the water that condenses in the small bowl? Is the water still purified?

THE SCIENCE BEHIND THE FUN

The sun's energy evaporates the water in the large bowl, turning it from a liquid into a gas. As the water vapor rises and comes into contact with the plastic, it cools and condenses back into droplets of liquid water. These grow and flow down the dip in the plastic wrap and fall into the small bowl. The salt stays dissolved in the water in the large bowl.

A solar "still" uses the same science on a larger scale. Impure water is collected outdoors under clear plastic or glass. Sunlight evaporates the water, and the vapor is directed through an underground pipe. There, it condenses on the cool inside surface and drips down to be collected and removed for use. This leaves behind impurities and eliminates micro-organisms to produce pure, distilled drinking water.

CONSTRUCTION PAPER SUN PRINTS

TOOLS & MATERIALS

- cardboard
- utility knife or box cutter
- blue or other dark colors of construction paper
- leaves
- plastic sheet protectors
- 8" × 10" (20 cm × 25 cm) picture frame (or larger)
- scissors

SAFETY TIPS, HINTS & TRICKS

- This lab takes place over the course of a couple days and requires an undisturbed, very sunny location to work.
- To get a larger piece of plastic from a single sheet protector, use scissors to cut off the bottom and hole-punched sides, then unfold and flatten it.

Create gorgeous art pieces using only leaves, construction paper, and the sun.

TIME: 2 TO 3 DAYS

Fig. 4: Frame and proudly display your natural artwork.

PROTOCOL

STEP 1: Lay a sheet of construction paper on the carboard and have an adult help you cut the cardboard to size with the utility knife or box cutter. (Fig. 1)

STEP 2: Gather leaves that have interesting shapes or that are composed of many smaller leaf components. Lay them on the construction paper. (Fig. 2)

STEP 3: Place the plastic sheet protector over the leaves. Remove the glass, back, and any inserts from the frame and put them aside. Set the frame on top of the sheet protector. (Fig. 3)

STEP 4: Place your setup in a very sunny spot for at least 24 hours and up to 48 hours (or even longer). Check on your sun print a few times a day, but be careful not to move it. Do you notice any changes in the paper?

STEP 5: After a couple days, remove the frame, sheet protector, and leaves to reveal your print. There should be darker silhouettes on the paper from the leaves and the frame.

Fig. 1: Prep your paper and cardboard.

Fig. 2: Leaves with unique shapes and lots of detail are the best to use.

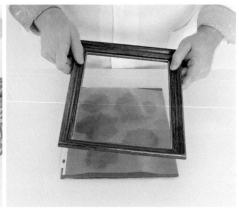

Fig. 3: The sheet protector lets sunlight through. The frame holds everything in place.

STEP 6: Reassemble the frame and trim the sun print to fit inside. For a more striking effect, put your print in a larger frame to reveal the darker border. (Fig. 4)

CREATIVE ENRICHMENT: DID YOU KNOW?

In addition to acting like a wave, light can also act like a particle. In 1905, Albert Einstein proposed that a beam of light is a collection of "wave packets" known as *photons*. In quantum mechanics, the smallest bit of something—a quantum—can be described as having "wave-particle duality." A photon is a single quantum of light.

THE SCIENCE BEHIND THE FUN

When exposed to sunlight, construction paper fades through a process called *photodegradation* (FO-to-deg-ruh-DEY-shun)—the breaking down of a substance with light, usually in the presence of oxygen and/or water vapor.

When a pigment molecule absorbs a photon, it excites an electron to a higher energy state. Most of the time, this energy is released as heat, but sometimes, it breaks a chemical bond or causes a reaction with another molecule (or both). This changes the molecule's structure, its absorption and reflection properties, and ultimately its color.

UV radiation has greater energy than visible light and is more likely to degrade pigment molecules. For outdoor signs and banners, UV-blocking coatings are applied to extend the life of the dyes.

UNDERSTANDING PHOTOSYNTHESIS

TOOLS & MATERIALS

- ⊘ green leaves
- ⊘ isopropyl (rubbing) alcohol
- ⊘ short glass or beaker
- ⊘ plastic wrap
- ⊘ glass bowl or shallow dish
- ⊘ water
- ⊘ coffee filter
- ⊘ scissors
- ⊘ pencil
- ⊘ tape

SAFETY TIPS, HINTS & TRICKS

- ⊘ For best results, choose leaves that turn vibrant colors in the fall, such as maple or aspen.
- ⊘ For safety's sake, have an adult help with the rubbing alcohol.

Extract pigments from leaves with alcohol and learn how plants use chlorophyll, sunlight, carbon dioxide, and water to make sugars and oxygen.

TIME: 1 TO 2 DAYS

Fig. 3: Bands of pigment separate along the strip of coffee filter paper.

PROTOCOL

STEP 1: Tear up the leaves into small pieces and/or grind them up using a mortar and pestle, if you have one. Put the leaf matter in the glass or beaker and add enough rubbing alcohol to submerge it. Cover the glass with plastic wrap to keep the alcohol from evaporating.

STEP 2: Fill the bottom of the bowl with very hot tap water. Place the glass in the bowl and swirl the mixture every 15 minutes for about an hour. Then let it sit (as long as overnight) until the alcohol turns bright green. (Fig. 1)

STEP 3: Flatten the coffee filter and cut it into 1-inch (2.5 cm) strips. Tape a single long strip to the pencil and suspend it over the glass so the end of the strip just touches the surface of the alcohol solution. Twist the pencil to shorten the strip, as needed. (Fig. 2)

Fig. 1: Swirl and warm the mixture in a hot water bath.

Fig. 2: The paper should just touch the top of the alcohol solution.

Fig. 4: Tiny oxygen bubbles form on the leaf's surface as photosynthesis continues.

STEP 4: After about 30 minutes, observe the bands of color that form on the filter strip. Can you see other pigments besides green? What do you observe after 60 minutes? After 90 minutes? (Fig. 3)

CREATIVE ENRICHMENT: REAL-TIME PHOTOSYNTHESIS MINI LAB

Choose a large green leaf and use small stones to submerge it in a bowl of room-temperature water. Place the bowl in direct sunlight for about an hour. What do you observe? (Fig. 4)

THE SCIENCE BEHIND THE FUN

Green plants use sunlight to make food from carbon dioxide and water through a process called *photosynthesis* (FO-toe-SIN-thuh-sis). The green pigment chlorophyll harnesses the energy of blue and red wavelengths and transfers electrons from water to carbon dioxide to produce carbohydrates, such as glucose, which feed the plant (and us). Breathable oxygen gas is released as a by-product. (Fig. 5)

We used rubbing alcohol in this lab to extract pigments from the leaves' cells. The resulting solution is green because of chlorophyll, but other pigments are also present. The coffee filter absorbs the solution and draws it upward. Pigments are carried along at different rates depending on how they dissolve in the alcohol and separate into bands of color.

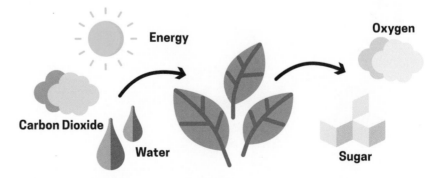

Fig. 5: The chemical process of photosynthesis

UNIT 3
THE CLOUDS & THE RAIN

The water cycle is the process by which water constantly moves around the planet. It has four basic stages: evaporation, condensation, precipitation, and collection.

The heat of the sun causes water in oceans, lakes, rivers, ice, and soil to turn into water vapor—to evaporate—and rise into the atmosphere, where it cools and condenses into tiny droplets of liquid water (or freezes directly into ice crystals), forming clouds.

These droplets and crystals are light enough to stay aloft, but as they grow larger, they become heavier, and gravity pulls them down as precipitation—rain, snow, hail, and sleet that falls to the Earth. Some of this water soaks into the soil and becomes groundwater, while the rest collects in oceans, lakes, rivers, and other bodies to be evaporated all over again.

In this unit, you'll take a deep dive into the water cycle. You'll start with a simple experiment demonstrating how temperature, air movement, and surface area directly impact evaporation, and you'll build a fun, swingable device with a milk carton to determine how much water vapor is in the air.

You'll make a cloud right in a jar and build an instrument that sounds just like rain. Then you'll collect rainwater directly from the sky and report on the amount of precipitation and the pH level of the water to determine if you have acid rain. You'll finish out the unit by discovering how the sun makes rainbows (and how the moon makes moonbows!) and then you'll make your own.

Lab 16

EVAPORATION STATION

TOOLS & MATERIALS

- 2 dry dish sponges
- 2 small plates
- measuring cup
- water
- desk lamp with a lightbulb that gives off heat
- electric fan
- small drinking glass
- calculator
- pie pan or shallow dish
- ruler

SAFETY TIPS, HINTS & TRICKS

- Patience is the key with this lab. Some tests can take many hours or even multiple days to get final results.
- Incandescent lightbulbs give off heat while LED and fluorescent bulbs do not.
- Be sure that the only variable in each experiment is the factor being measured. Try to make all other elements of the environment the same for both sponges.

Experiment with the effects of temperature, wind, and surface area on the evaporation of water.

TIME: 2 TO 3 DAYS

Water evaporates off of a hot spring in Yellowstone National Park, Wyoming, United States.

PROTOCOL

STEP 1: Start by testing the effect of temperature on evaporation. Place each sponge on a small plate. Pour ⅛ cup (30 ml) of water onto each one. The sponges should absorb all the water. (Fig. 1)

STEP 2: Place one sponge under the lamp and turn it on. Place the other at room temperature, away from any heat source. (Fig. 2)

STEP 3: Observe and touch the sponges every 30 minutes to an hour. How does their wetness change? Write down your observations. Shorten the time between measurements as the sponges dry. Which sponge dried faster, and why?

Fig. 1: Add the same amount of water to each sponge.

Fig. 2: Shine a lamp on one of the sponges.

Fig. 3: Point a fan at one of the sponges.

STEP 4: Next, test the effect of wind. Plate and wet the sponges again as in Step 1. Set one sponge in front of the fan, about 6 inches (15 cm) away, and turn on the fan so that it blows on the sponge. (Fig. 3)

STEP 5: Set the other sponge in the same room but out of the path of the fan. Take measurements of the wetness of each sponge as in Step 3. Compare the time it took for the lamp to dry the sponge and the time it took the fan. Which is faster?

STEP 6: Lastly, test the effect of surface area. Pour ⅛ cup (30 ml) of water into a small glass and measure its diameter with a ruler.

STEP 7: Calculate the surface area of the water by finding the area of a circle. Using a calculator, multiply *pi* (π) by the radius squared ($\pi \times r^2$), where $\pi = 3.1416$ and $r = $ ½ of the diameter of the glass.

STEP 8: Pour ⅛ cup (30 ml) of water into the pie pan or shallow dish and measure its diameter. Calculate the surface area of the water using the equation from Step 7. (Fig. 4)

STEP 9: Place the glass and pan or dish where they won't be disturbed. Observe them a number of times each day and notice how much water has evaporated. Which evaporates faster, and why?

Fig. 4: Fill a glass and a pie pan or shallow dish with the same amount of water.

CONTINUED

CREATIVE ENRICHMENT: TAKING IT FURTHER

1. Increase or decrease the wattage of the light bulb or the speed of the fan. Place the lamp or fan closer or further away from the sponge. How does this change the speed of evaporation?

2. Try this lab with isopropyl (rubbing) alcohol or with ethyl alcohol (ethanol) found in vodka or gin. Get assistance from an adult and do this in a place with good ventilation. What differences and similarities do you observe?

THE SCIENCE BEHIND THE FUN

In this lab, you tested temperature, moving air, and surface area and should have observed that an increase in any of these increases the rate of evaporation.

Higher temperatures give water molecules more energy, making them more likely to change from a liquid to a gas. Water's boiling point is 212°F (100°C), but it doesn't have to boil to evaporate. Evaporation is always happening right at the surface of any body of water where it interacts with air and sunlight at the molecular level.

Moving air acts to push away water vapor directly above a body of water. This brings in dryer air, which accepts more water vapor before it is also pushed away. As more dry air blows in, the rate of evaporation speeds up. An increase in surface area increases how much water is touching the air, also resulting in more evaporation.

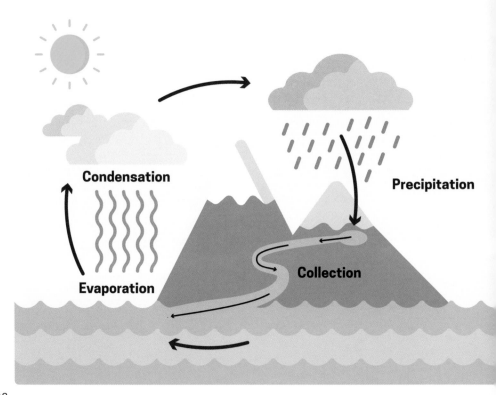

MAKE RAINBOWS

TOOLS & MATERIALS

- ⊙ wide drinking glass or beaker
- ⊙ water
- ⊙ small mirror, such as a compact or makeup mirror
- ⊙ flashlight
- ⊙ scissors
- ⊙ white paper
- ⊙ tape
- ⊙ garden hose
- ⊙ spray nozzle

Fig. 6: A gorgeous double rainbow appears in Capitol Reef National Park, Utah.

You can use simple items from around the house to make your own rainbows!

TIME: 30 MINUTES

SAFETY TIPS, HINTS & TRICKS

- ⊙ Broken glass in water can be dangerous, so have an adult handle the mirror.
- ⊙ The flashlight should emit a strong, focused beam of white light.

PROTOCOL

STEP 1: Fill the glass or beaker halfway with water and have an adult place the mirror in the water at an angle.

STEP 2: Turn off the lights and shine the flashlight at the mirror through the side of the glass. (Fig. 1)

CONTINUED

Fig. 1: Angle a small mirror in a glass of water and shine a flashlight on it.

Fig. 2: Cover only half of the bottom of the glass with a piece of paper.

Fig. 3: The glass gives the light a rounded shape.

STEP 3: Look for reflections of the light as a rainbow on the wall or ceiling. You may have to shift the flashlight, mirror, or glass to find the correct angle. What order are the rainbow's colors in? How is this different from a rainbow in nature?

STEP 4: Remove the mirror from the water. Cut a small rectangular piece of white paper and tape it over one half of the bottom of the glass. (Fig. 2)

STEP 5: Place a sheet of white paper on the surface and hold the glass over it.

STEP 6: Turn off the lights and shine the flashlight down through the glass. (Fig. 3)

STEP 7: Move the glass and/or flashlight up or down, adjusting the distance and angle until you focus a rainbow on the paper. What order are the colors in? How are they different, and why?

STEP 8: Attach a spray nozzle to a garden hose. Attach the hose to an outdoor faucet and turn on the water.

STEP 9: Press the lever on the spray nozzle just enough to produce a very fine mist. Position yourself and the spray toward the sun and look into the mist. What do you see? What order are the colors in? How is this different from the glass experiments? (Fig. 4)

Fig. 4: Use a garden hose to spray mist into the sun to make another rainbow.

Fig. 5: A moonbow appears above Victoria Falls on the Zambezi River between Zimbabwe and Zambia in southern Africa.

CREATIVE ENRICHMENT: MOONBOW MINI LAB

While extremely rare in nature, "moonbows" do happen. They occur when the sky is clear, the moon is full, and there's lots of moisture in the air. Moonbows are fainter than regular rainbows and most often appear as white arches. (Fig. 5)

When there is a very clear night accompanied by a full moon, go outside and make mist with your garden hose and spray nozzle like you did in Step 9. Can you make a moonbow of your own in the moonlight?

THE SCIENCE BEHIND THE FUN

In nature, rainbows form when sunlight passes through water droplets suspended in the air. The light *refracts* (bends) as it enters, reflects off the droplet's inside surface, and refracts again upon leaving. The colors of light fan out, with red bending the least and appearing at the top and violet bending the most and appearing at the bottom.

A double rainbow occurs when the light reflects a second time off the inside front surface of the water droplets and refracts out the back side. The outer bow is much fainter than the inner one and the colors are reversed. (Fig. 6)

The spray nozzle models what happens in nature as the mist floats and falls slowly through the air, refracting and reflecting light that shines through it. This also demonstrates how, in order to see a rainbow, you have to be in the right place at the right time and looking at the correct angle.

BUILD A HYGROMETER

TOOLS & MATERIALS

- empty milk carton
- paper
- tape
- large nail or awl
- a few yards of string or twine
- stapler
- 2 small thermometers
- cotton ball
- eyedropper

SAFETY TIPS, HINTS & TRICKS

- The milk carton should be pint- or quart-sized. Be sure it is thoroughly clean and dry.
- Use small glass alcohol thermometers, the ones with a thin line of red or blue liquid inside. Be sure you know how to read one.
- Do the swinging part of this lab outdoors in a wide-open space so that you have enough room to safely spin your device.

Make a wet-and-dry-bulb thermometer and use it to determine the air's relative humidity.

TIME: 30 MINUTES

Fig. 4: Stay clear of any objects or people while swinging your device.

PROTOCOL

STEP 1: Wrap the milk carton with paper and tape so the thermometers are easier to read.

STEP 2: Have an adult use the nail or awl to punch two holes in the top of the milk carton. Thread a 6-foot (2 m) piece of string through the holes, tie the ends together securely to form a loop, and close up the top of the carton with the stapler or tape. (Fig. 1)

STEP 3: Cover the bulb of one thermometer with a cotton ball and tie it in place with a piece of string. (Fig.2)

STEP 4: Tape each thermometer to opposite sides of the milk carton. Make sure they're secure. Use the eyedropper to saturate the cotton ball with water. (Fig. 3)

STEP 5: Take your hygrometer outside to a clear open space and swing it around for 60 seconds. (Fig. 4)

STEP 6: Take a reading of the two thermometers, starting with the one with the cotton ball. Write down both values.

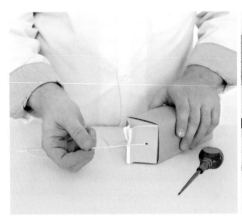

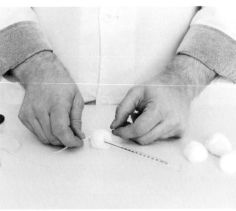

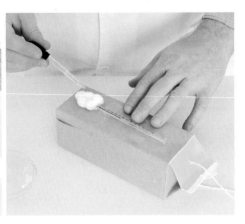

Fig. 1: Create at least a 3-foot (1 m) handle out of string.

Fig. 2: Wrap one thermometer in cotton secured with string.

Fig. 3: Attach the thermometers with tape and add water to the cotton ball.

STEP 7: Enter your values into an online relative humidity calculator (see the links in the Resources & References section, page 140). You'll also need to enter the atmospheric pressure, which you can get from the weather report. What is the relative humidity?

CREATIVE ENRICHMENT: DEW POINT MINI LAB

Put a glass thermometer in a clean, empty aluminum can and fill the can halfway with room-temperature water. Take a temperature reading. Slowly cool the water by adding small bits of crushed ice and gently stirring with the thermometer. As the ice melts, notice how the temperature drops. When you see the first signs of condensation forming on the outside of the can, take another temperature reading. This is the dew point.

THE SCIENCE BEHIND THE FUN

A hygrometer is any instrument used to measure the amount of water vapor in the air or soil. Relative humidity is the actual amount of water vapor present in the air compared to the amount that *could* be in the air at a certain temperature (expressed as a percentage).

The device you built in this lab is specifically called a *sling psychrometer* (sy-KRAH-meh-ter), which uses two thermometers—one that's dry and one that's kept moist—and is spun manually on a "sling" to determine the humidity.

After swinging your psychrometer, you'll notice a lower reading on the thermometer with the cotton ball (the wet bulb) than the thermometer on its own (the dry bulb). When you swing it, the water in the cotton ball evaporates and reduces the temperature. The drier the air, the easier it is for water to evaporate, and the bigger the difference in the thermometer readings.

A CLOUD IN A JAR

Lab 19

TOOLS & MATERIALS

- ⊘ glass jar
- ⊘ black paper
- ⊘ scissors
- ⊘ tape
- ⊘ warm tap water
- ⊘ ice cubes
- ⊘ small metal bowl
- ⊘ matches
- ⊘ flashlight

You don't need the sky to make a cloud—just a jar!

TIME: 20 MINUTES

Fig. 4: Shine the flashlight into the jar to make the cloud more visible.

SAFETY TIPS, HINTS & TRICKS

- ⊘ Long matches work best for this lab and prevent burned fingers!
- ⊘ Since fire is involved, you'll need an adult's assistance.
- ⊘ The bowl should be large enough to cover the jar's opening.
- ⊘ If you don't have a small metal bowl, the lid of the jar turned upside down works too.

PROTOCOL

STEP 1: Cut a piece of black paper to fit around half the jar and tape it in place. (Fig. 1)

STEP 2: Add about 2 inches (5 cm) of warm tap water to the jar. Fill the small metal bowl with ice cubes.

STEP 3: Have an adult light a match and hold it in the jar for 3 to 5 seconds. (Fig. 2)

STEP 4: Drop the match into the water to extinguish it. Immediately cover the mouth of the jar with the metal bowl full of ice. (Fig. 3)

Fig. 1: The black paper acts as a dark background so you can see the cloud.

Fig. 2: Let the match burn for just a little bit.

Fig. 3: Put the match out in the water and put the bowl of ice on the jar.

STEP 5: Look through the side of the jar, toward the black paper background. What do you notice?

STEP 6: As the cloud forms and gets larger, turn off the lights and shine a flashlight into the jar. (Fig. 4)

STEP 7: Once a sizeable cloud has formed, take the bowl off the mouth of the jar. What happens to the cloud?

CREATIVE ENRICHMENT: DID YOU KNOW?

Different types of clouds get their names from their shapes and where they are found in the sky. Cirrus (SEER-uss) clouds form high up and appear wispy and feathery because they're made of tiny floating ice crystals. Cumulus (KYOO-myoo-luss) clouds are middle clouds, shaped like giant cotton balls. Stratus (STRA-tuss) clouds are low and cover the sky like sheets. Clouds that form very near the Earth's surface are called fog.

THE SCIENCE BEHIND THE FUN

In this lab, water vapor rises from the warm water in the jar. You can't see it, but at the water's surface, heat excites molecules to overcome surface tension and air pressure to go from liquid to gas.

As the water vapor encounters the cold metal of the bowl of ice, it cools, and the particles of smoke from the match provide tiny surfaces on which the water can condense. As more vapor becomes liquid, the cloud grows and becomes visible. When the bowl is removed, water stops condensing, and warm water vapor pushes the cloud up and out of the jar.

MAKE A RAIN STICK

Lab 20

TOOLS & MATERIALS

- ⊘ long cardboard tube (or many shorter tubes taped together)
- ⊘ brown kraft paper
- ⊘ pencil
- ⊘ scissors
- ⊘ tape
- ⊘ aluminum foil
- ⊘ small, dry material (lentils, beans, rice, popping corn)
- ⊘ measuring cup
- ⊘ funnel (optional)
- ⊘ crayons, markers, construction or craft paper, glue, and other art supplies (optional)

SAFETY TIPS, HINTS & TRICKS

- ⊘ Your tube should be about 1½ to 2 inches (3.5 to 5 cm) in diameter.
- ⊘ The longer the tube, the better the sound of your rain stick. Use a wrapping paper tube or a number of paper towel or toilet paper tubes taped together in a long column at least 3 feet (1 m) long.

Capture the sound of falling rain in this simple instrument you can craft yourself.

TIME: 1 HOUR

Fig. 5: Turn your rain stick over to hear the soothing sound of rain!

PROTOCOL

STEP 1: Trace the end of the tube onto a piece of kraft paper. Around this circle, draw another circle that is twice as big, then draw four to six equidistant connecting lines between the two circles. Do this twice.

STEP 2: Cut out one of the bigger circles and cut in along the lines to the edge of the smaller circle. Tape this cap to one end of the cardboard tube to seal it. (Fig. 1)

STEP 3: Cut three pieces of aluminum foil that are each 1½ to 2 times as long as your tube and about 6 inches (15 cm) wide.

Fig. 1: Trace and draw two spoked circles. Cut one out and use it to seal one end of the tube.

Fig. 2: Cut, crunch, and spiral the aluminum foil.

Fig. 3: Insert your foil "springs" into the tube.

Fig. 4: You'll hear the sound of rain as you add the lentils, rice, or beans.

STEP 4: Scrunch up the strips of aluminum foil into long, thin ropes and twist each one into a spiral shape that will fit inside the cardboard tube. (Fig. 2)

STEP 5: Push the three aluminum foil spirals into the cardboard tube. (Fig. 3)

STEP 6: Carefully pour in about ½ cup (80 g) of your dried material. Use a funnel to make it easier. (Fig. 4)

STEP 7: Cut out the second brown kraft paper cap. With tape, use it to seal off the other end of your tube, encasing the foil and dry material inside.

STEP 8: Wrap your rain stick with more brown kraft paper or colorful craft or construction paper. Decorate the outside with crayons and markers, stickers and embellishments, or paper cutouts.

STEP 9: Turn your rain stick over and listen carefully. What do you hear? (Fig. 5)

CREATIVE ENRICHMENT: TAKING IT FURTHER

- How do different kinds, mixtures, or amounts of dried materials inside the rain stick change its sound?

- How does using more or fewer aluminum foil spirals affect the sound?

THE SCIENCE BEHIND THE FUN

Rain sticks were most likely invented by the Mapuche (mah-POO-cheh)—indigenous people of present-day south-central Chile and southwestern Argentina—who believed the tools had the power to bring rain when "played."

Traditional rain sticks are made from sun-dried cactus. The spines are removed and then carefully driven back into the cactus cylinder in a helix pattern. Pebbles, beans, or other small, hard materials are sealed inside.

When the stick is turned vertically, the material falls to one end, striking the spines (or in the case of this lab, the foil) and making a sound like falling rain. Similar instruments made from other materials can be found all over the world.

MEASURE RAINFALL

TOOLS & MATERIALS

- empty 2-liter plastic bottle
- utility or craft knife
- clean rocks or glass marbles
- electrical tape
- masking tape
- water
- ruler
- permanent marker

SAFETY TIPS, HINTS & TRICKS

- Cutting a plastic bottle with a sharp knife can be awkward and dangerous. Have an adult do this step.

Measure how much rain falls by making your very own rain gauge from a recycled bottle.

TIME: 1 DAY

Fig. 4: Choose an ideal spot where your rain gauge can sit undisturbed.

PROTOCOL

STEP 1: Remove the cap from the bottle. Have an adult use the knife to neatly and carefully cut the top off the bottle. Save the top for Step 3. (Fig. 1)

STEP 2: Place the rocks or marbles in the bottom of the bottle in a layer 1 to 2 inches (2.5 to 5 cm) thick. This will keep the gauge from blowing over.

STEP 3: Place the cut top from Step 1 in the bottle with its neck pointing downward to make a funnel. Line up the cut edges and use electrical tape to connect them. (Fig. 2)

STEP 4: Attach a long piece of masking tape vertically on the side of the bottle. Make sure the tape is very straight. Make a horizontal mark on the tape, just above the rocks or marbles. Label this "0" to act as the gauge's bottom and the starting measurement.

STEP 5: Line up the end of the ruler with the bottle's "0" line and make a mark every ¼ or ½ inch (6 mm or 1 cm) along the piece of tape. Number the inches (cm). (Fig. 3)

Fig. 1: Have an adult cut the top of the bottle off below the "shoulders."

Fig. 2: Tape the top of the bottle upside down like a funnel inside the gauge.

Fig. 3: Create a masking-tape ruler on the outside of the bottle.

STEP 6: When there's rain in the forecast, add water to your gauge to the "0" mark. Then place it outdoors on a level surface that's open to the sky. (Fig. 4)

STEP 7: After 24 hours, record the water level in your gauge. Check your local weather to see how closely your measurement matches the reported rainfall for the day. Save the water from this lab for Lab 22.

CREATIVE ENRICHMENT: DID YOU KNOW?

Petrichor (PEH-trih-kor) is the scent produced when rain strikes the dry ground. It comes from an oil produced by certain plants during dry periods that is absorbed by clay and rocks as well as another compound called geosmin (JEE-ohz-muhn), which is a by-product of bacteria in the soil. Some scientists believe humans notice and enjoy this distinctive smell because, for our ancestors, it indicated the arrival of rainy weather needed for survival.

THE SCIENCE BEHIND THE FUN

When it rains, what happens to the water when it reaches the ground depends on five factors.

- **Rate of Rainfall:** A lot of rain in a short period of time runs off instead of soaking into the ground.
- **Soil Conditions:** Loose, sandy soils absorb water better than denser soils containing clay.
- **Topography:** Rain falling on uneven land flows downhill, gathers in bodies of water, or soaks into the ground.
- **Vegetation Density:** Plants slow the speed of flowing water and hold soil in place.
- **Urbanization:** Buildings, roads, and parking lots keep water from seeping into the ground, and flooding can result.

The portion of precipitation that reaches streams in the United States every year produces an average flow of about 1.2 trillion gallons (4.5 trillion L) a day. If only a third of that could be collected and stored, it would supply more than enough daily water for the United States' almost 330 million people.

ACID RAIN TEST

TOOLS & MATERIALS

- ⊙ large head of purple cabbage
- ⊙ sharp knife
- ⊙ blender
- ⊙ hot water
- ⊙ sieve
- ⊙ cheesecloth or paper towels
- ⊙ large bowl
- ⊙ coffee filters
- ⊙ baking pan
- ⊙ aluminum foil or wax paper
- ⊙ electric fan or hair dryer (optional)
- ⊙ eyedropper
- ⊙ disposable gloves (optional)

SAFETY TIPS, HINTS & TRICKS

- ⊙ Have an adult handle the knife and operate the blender.
- ⊙ To keep from temporarily dyeing your fingers purple, you can wear protective gloves for this lab.
- ⊙ To prevent contamination, always be sure to drip the rain sample on the testing paper rather than putting the paper in the sample.

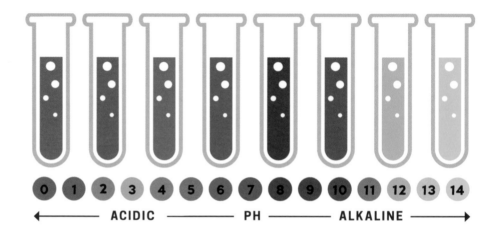

| 0 | 1 | 2 | 3 | 4 | 5 | 6 | 7 | 8 | 9 | 10 | 11 | 12 | 13 | 14 |

← ACIDIC ———— PH ———— ALKALINE →

Make simple litmus paper from cabbage juice and coffee filters to measure the pH of rain.

Fig. 4: The spectrum of cabbage juice indicator

TIME: 1 TO 2 HOURS

PROTOCOL

STEP 1: Have an adult chop up half of the head of cabbage and put it in a blender with 3 cups (710 ml) of very hot water. Blend it on high for 1 to 2 minutes.

STEP 2: Line a sieve with cheesecloth or a single layer of paper towels and set it in the bowl. Strain the mixture to separate the chopped-up cabbage from the liquid. Discard or compost the solids and let the liquid cool completely in the bowl. (Fig. 1)

STEP 3: Cover the sheet pan with foil or wax paper. Soak a coffee filter in the cabbage juice for about 30 seconds and place it on the sheet pan to dry completely. Make as many as you'd like. See Lab 16 (page 52) for ways to speed up the drying process. (Fig. 2)

STEP 4: Once they're dry, cut your dyed filters into 1-inch (2.5 cm) strips. (Fig. 3)

Fig. 1: Separate the purple liquid from the puréed cabbage.

Fig. 2: Soak the filters and dry them on a baking pan.

Fig. 3: Cut your litmus paper into strips.

STEP 5: Collect rainwater in a clean container, directly from the sky, so your results are not affected by contaminants from the ground or other surfaces. You can use the water you collected in Lab 21.

STEP 6: Use an eyedropper to test the sample. Drop a small amount of water onto a strip of the paper. What do you observe? What color does the paper turn? What is the pH of your sample? How does your rainwater compare to tap water? (Fig. 4)

CREATIVE ENRICHMENT: RESPIRATION MINI LAB

You can use cabbage juice to show that there's carbon dioxide in the air you exhale. Fill a glass with cold water and add a bit of cabbage juice. Place a straw in the water and blow bubbles into the liquid for about a minute. Do you notice a change in the color? What do you think is happening, and why?

THE SCIENCE BEHIND THE FUN

In water, there is always a small number of molecules that split, lose a hydrogen atom, and become hydroxide ions ($OH-$). Other molecules gain the lost hydrogen atoms to form hydronium ions (H_3O+), also known as hydrogen ions ($H+$) or just protons. In pure water (which is "neutral") there is an equal number of both ions.

When an acid dissolves in water, it shifts this balance so there are many more hydrogen ions than hydroxide ions. An alkaline substance (or base) shifts the balance the other way as it "soaks up" hydrogen ions, resulting in many more hydroxide ions.

Cabbage gets its vibrant color from pigments called *anthocyanins* (an-thow-SAI-uh-ninz). Changes in the level of acidity or alkalinity (the pH) change their shape, which changes their color, resulting in the spectrum seen in Fig. 4.

In the mini lab, carbon dioxide in your breath dissolves in the cold liquid, forms carbonic acid, lowers the pH of the liquid, and turns it pink. Similarly, sulfur and nitrogen oxides—waste gases from burning coal and other fossil fuels—mix with water in the atmosphere to form sulfuric and nitric acid, which fall as acid rain.

UNIT 4
THE WINDS THAT BLOW

Wind occurs in many different forms all over the Earth—from strong thunderstorm gusts to gentle coastal breezes to massive global air flows. Wind is an important means of transportation not only for humans but also for birds, insects, and even seeds, which can travel thousands of miles on it.

Each of the Earth's hemispheres is home to three massive, gear-like bands of circulating air called the Hadley, Ferrel, and polar cells. Within these circulation cells, global winds blow, influenced by differences in the Earth's absorption of the sun's energy across climate zones. Following the boundaries, or *fronts*, of hot and cold air between the cells are the *jet streams*—narrow bands of strong wind in the upper troposphere that move weather systems from west to east.

In this unit, you'll start by learning about convection currents and how huge masses of swirling air are the foundation of the Earth's weather. You'll experiment with the sea breeze/land breeze cycle that defines winds in coastal areas, and you'll build simple tools to measure wind speed and direction while you fly paper airplanes and keep a kite aloft. Finally, you'll demonstrate how the wind erodes the land, blowing away valuable nutrients and topsoil while stirring up dust and pollution that can travel great distances from their source.

You'll discover that whatever its form or function, the wind has a huge influence on life on this planet, defining its past, present, and future.

CONVECTION CURRENTS

TOOLS & MATERIALS

- ⊘ pan or kettle
- ⊘ stovetop
- ⊘ water
- ⊘ large glass container
- ⊘ small jar or glass
- ⊘ food coloring
- ⊘ plastic wrap
- ⊘ rubber band
- ⊘ kitchen tongs
- ⊘ knife

SAFETY TIPS, HINTS & TRICKS

- ⊘ This lab uses very hot water and a sharp knife—adult supervision is required.
- ⊘ If you don't want to heat the water on the stove, put it in a mug and heat it in the microwave instead.
- ⊘ Cover your work surface with newspaper to protect it from moisture and the dye in the food coloring.

Use hot and cold water and a little food dye to model convection.

TIME: 1 HOUR

Fig. 4: Convection currents occur when the cold water and dyed hot water start to mix.

PROTOCOL

STEP 1: Ask an adult to heat the water to almost boiling in a pan or a kettle on the stove. Be careful when handling the hot liquid.

STEP 2: Fill the large glass container about three-quarters full of cold tap water. Fill the small jar or glass almost all the way to the top with the hot water and add 15 to 20 drops of food coloring. (Fig. 1)

STEP 3: Cover the mouth of the jar or glass with plastic wrap and secure it with a rubber band. (Fig. 2)

STEP 4: Use the tongs to submerge the jar or glass of hot water in the container of cold tap water. (Fig. 3)

STEP 5: Pierce the plastic wrap with a knife. What do you notice? Observe your setup every 5 minutes for up to an hour. What happens to the hot, colored water? (Fig. 4)

Fig. 1: Add cold, clear water to the large container and hot, colored water to the small jar.

Fig. 2: Use a rubber band to secure the plastic wrap.

Fig. 3: Carefully place the jar or glass in the cold water.

CREATIVE ENRICHMENT: COLD CURRENTS MINI LAB

Mix cold tap water with blue food coloring in a measuring cup. Pour it into an ice cube tray and freeze it. Fill a large, clear glass with room-temperature tap water and let it sit for about 30 minutes. Then, carefully drop in one of the blue ice cubes and watch what happens. How does this compare to the hot water experiment?

THE SCIENCE BEHIND THE FUN

Convection transfers heat through the motion of a fluid, such as water or air. On our planet, convection in the oceans creates currents and sustains life while convection in the molten rock beneath the Earth's crust moves the tectonic plates. Convection currents of air influence the weather. Constantly moving, large-scale atmospheric cells keep the clouds aloft and drive continual circulation at the Earth's surface that we call wind.

In the lab, hot, colored water is released and rises to the surface while cooler water is pulled down to replace it. The red water then cools and sinks down while the cooler water warms and rises up. This process continues until the water is evenly heated and the food coloring is evenly distributed.

In the mini lab, the same thing occurs, except the cold water has been dyed instead of the hot, which shows more clearly how cooler fluid descends.

FEEL THE BREEZE

TOOLS & MATERIALS

- ⊘ 2 glass baking dishes of the same size
- ⊘ sand
- ⊘ oven
- ⊘ oven mitts
- ⊘ potholders or trivets
- ⊘ ice
- ⊘ water
- ⊘ thermometer (instant read is best)
- ⊘ incense, sage stick, or a candle
- ⊘ matches or lighter
- ⊘ large cardboard box (optional)

SAFETY TIPS, HINTS & TRICKS

- ⊘ Since this lab involves fire and uses an oven, adult supervision is required.
- ⊘ To block any drafts that might affect your results, you can cut two adjacent long sides out of a large rectangular cardboard box and place it over your setup.
- ⊘ If you don't have glass baking dishes, ceramic or metal will work as well.

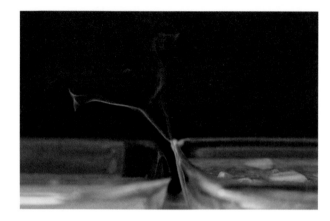

Show why it's windy at the beach using materials you can find in your kitchen.

TIME: 30 MINUTES

Fig. 4: The stream of smoke moves with the breeze.

PROTOCOL

STEP 1: Preheat the oven to 300°F (150°C) and then choose a flat surface in a location without wind or other drafts. If necessary, use the cut cardboard box to protect your setup.

STEP 2: Pour a ½-inch (1 cm) layer of sand into one baking dish and warm it in the oven for 5 to 8 minutes. You want the temperature of the sand to be between 150°F and 175°F (70°C to 80°C). (Fig. 1)

STEP 3: Have an adult light the incense, sage, or candle and blow it out. Hold or place it where you'll do your experiment and observe the smoke. How does it flow? If the smoke doesn't stream straight up, try to block any drafts or choose a new location. (Fig. 2)

STEP 4: Fill the second dish halfway with ice and water and place it on your chosen surface.

STEP 5: Have an adult use oven mitts to remove the hot sand from the oven and place it on a potholder or trivet right next to the dish of ice water. Measure and record the temperature of each dish. (Fig. 3)

Fig. 1: Bake the sand to warm it up.

Fig. 2: Undisturbed smoke means you're ready to begin the experiment.

Fig. 3: Place the baking dishes side by side and take their temperatures.

STEP 6: Have an adult light the incense, sage, or candle again and blow it out. Hold the smoking tip in between the two dishes, right below or above the edge. Observe the movement of the smoke. Which direction does it flow now? (Fig. 4)

CREATIVE ENRICHMENT: TAKING IT FURTHER

1. Reverse the temperatures of the dishes—cool the sand and heat the water. What happens to the breeze?

2. Increase or decrease each dish's temperature. Is there a connection between the difference in temperature and the speed and direction of the smoke?

THE SCIENCE BEHIND THE FUN

Air above the hot sand heats up, expands, and starts to rise, causing a drop in pressure. Over the water, air cools, contracts, and sinks downward, increasing pressure. This difference in air pressure is what causes the movement of a "sea breeze."

Air from the high-pressure zone rushes into the low-pressure zone to fill in the empty space caused by the rising and expanding air. The sideways movement of smoke gives visual evidence of this flow. Greater differences between the water and sand temperatures produce stronger winds.

At night, the sea breeze turns into a land breeze. Because of its lower heat capacity, the sand cools quickly once the sun goes down. When the sand is colder than the water, the airflow pattern reverses.

BUILD AN ANEMOMETER

TOOLS & MATERIALS

- ⊙ 5 small paper cups
- ⊙ single-hole punch
- ⊙ 2 drinking straws
- ⊙ screwdriver or awl
- ⊙ cellophane tape
- ⊙ marker
- ⊙ unsharpened pencil with a new eraser
- ⊙ straight pin
- ⊙ vehicle and driver (for calibration)
- ⊙ stopwatch or other timer
- ⊙ calculator

SAFETY TIPS, HINTS & TRICKS

- ⊙ Ask an adult if you need help poking holes in the cups or pushing the pin into the pencil eraser.
- ⊙ The tape you use should be lightweight. When securing the cups, use the same amount on each, and use as little as possible in order to keep the device balanced.
- ⊙ Any person of driving age with a vehicle should be able to help you calibrate your device.

Combine cups, straws, and a pencil to make a simple device that measures wind speed.

TIME: 1 HOUR

Fig. 4: Your device should spin with minimal friction.

PROTOCOL

STEP 1: Make the central hub of your device by punching four evenly spaced holes around one of the cups. Each hole should be about ½ inch (1 cm) from the top edge.

STEP 2: Insert the straws through the holes so they overlap in the center in a cross. (Fig. 1)

STEP 3: Using the screwdriver or an awl, make a hole in the center of the bottom of the cup. The hole should be slightly larger than the diameter of your pencil.

STEP 4: Punch two holes in each remaining cup that are opposite each other and about ½ inch (1 cm) from the top rim.

STEP 5: Slide a cup onto each straw "arm." Position the cups so the opening of each one faces the bottom of the cup before it and tape them securely in place. With the marker, draw a large dot on the outside of one cup. (Fig. 2)

Fig. 1: Punch four equidistant holes in one cup and insert the straws so they intersect.

Fig. 2: Punch holes in each cup and attach them to the straws. Add a dot to one cup.

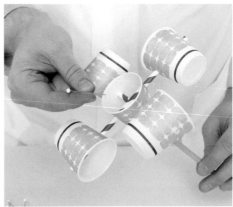

Fig. 3: A pin pushed into a pencil eraser is the axis around which the anemometer spins.

STEP 6: Insert the eraser end of the pencil through the hole in the bottom of the hub. Poke the straight pin through the center of the intersecting straws, into the eraser. (Fig. 3)

STEP 7: Hold the pencil in one hand and blow on your anemometer. The hub cup should spin freely and the intersected straws should spin around the pin without rubbing too much against the eraser. (Fig. 4)

STEP 8: Have a licensed driver with a car drive you down the street at 10 miles per hour (16.1 kph) on a calm day. To calibrate your anemometer, hold it out the window, start the stopwatch, and count the number of rotations (using the dot you drew) in 30 seconds. Do this a few times and average your measurements.

STEP 9: To measure wind speed, stand in one place and hold your anemometer in the air. Count the number of spins in 30 seconds. Use a calculator to divide this number by your value from Step 8 and multiply by 10 to get the speed in miles per hour (or by 16.1 to get kph).

CREATIVE ENRICHMENT: TAKING IT FURTHER

1. Compare your wind measurements with your local weather report. Do your values match?

2. Grab that licensed driver again and have them drive at whatever speed they want without telling you. Repeat Step 8 and use Step 9 to guess how fast they're driving!

THE SCIENCE BEHIND THE FUN

In this lab you made a "cup," or Robinson, anemometer (a-nuh-MAH-muh-tr), named after the Irish scientist who improved its design in 1846 with four half speres and mechanical wheels.

The cuplike shapes catch the wind and make the device spin. The number of spins in a given amount of time tells you how fast the wind is moving. It's a simple but effective measuring tool when compared to newer models that use lasers and ultrasonics.

MAKE A WEATHER VANE

TOOLS & MATERIALS

- 2 sturdy paper plates
- modeling clay
- pebbles or small rocks
- screwdriver or awl
- glue
- unsharpened pencil with a new eraser
- colored cardstock
- ruler
- scissors
- marker
- drinking straw
- tape
- straight pin
- navigational compass
- art supplies (optional)

SAFETY TIPS, HINTS & TRICKS

- You can also use plastic or foam plates, which tend to be more durable than paper.
- Get assistance from an adult when poking holes in the plates.
- Be as creative as you like with the look of your weather vane. Decorate the plates or wrap the pencil in colored tape.

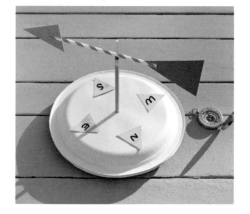

Fig. 4: Mount the arrow on the pencil eraser. Then take note of which way the arrow points in the wind.

Craft a fun paper-based tool to determine the wind direction.

TIME: 30 MINUTES

PROTOCOL

STEP 1: Place a golf-ball-sized piece of modeling clay in the center of one plate and press it down into a disc. Then pour a handful of pebbles around the clay. Press them evenly into the sides of the clay. This will help your weather vane stay standing. (Fig. 1)

STEP 2: Turn the other plate upside down and use the screwdriver or awl to poke a hole in the center, large enough to hold the pencil tightly. Next, run a small bead of glue around the rim of the plate with the hole and place it upside down on top of the plate with the clay and pebbles. Let the glue dry completely.

STEP 3: Cut out the following equilateral triangles from colored poster board or cardstock: one 4-inch (10-cm), one 3-inch (7.5-cm), and four 2-inch (5-cm).

Fig. 1: Weigh down your device with a large piece of clay and some pebbles.

Fig. 2: Add the compass direction points to the paper plate base.

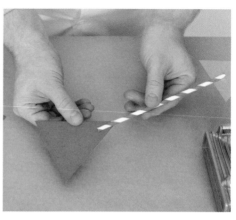

Fig. 3: Build the arrow with the last two triangles, a drinking straw, and some tape.

STEP 4: Write the following letters on a small triangle: N, E, S, W. To create compass points, glue the triangles pointing outward around the edge of the plate. Start at the top and move clockwise in this order: N (North), E (East), S (South), W (West). (Fig. 2)

STEP 5: Cut a 1-inch (2 cm) slit in the same position on either end of the drinking straw. Make an arrow by sliding one point of the larger triangle into one slit and the smaller triangle into the other slit. Secure these in place with a little tape. (Fig. 3)

STEP 6: Put a little glue on the wood end of the pencil and push it through the hole in the base into the clay, so it stands up straight. Let the glue dry completely.

STEP 7: Push the straight pin through the middle of the drinking straw arrow into the eraser of the pencil. Spin the arrow a few times to make sure it moves freely.

STEP 8: Go outside with your weather vane and place it on a flat, level surface. Using a compass, position the base so the N points northward. What do you observe when the wind blows? (Fig. 4)

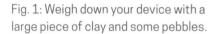

CREATIVE ENRICHMENT: DID YOU KNOW?

Weather vanes are probably the earliest instruments used to measure and predict the weather. The astronomer Andronicus built the first recorded weather vane for the Tower of the Winds in Athens.

THE SCIENCE BEHIND THE FUN

Instead of pointing in the direction that wind is traveling, weather vanes indicate the direction *from* which the wind originates. If your weather vane points to the N triangle, this means the wind is coming from the north and traveling in the southernly direction.

This is because the arrow's tail has a greater surface area than its point and is more affected by the wind's force. The tail creates greater drag (air resistance), and the wind forces it back as far as it will go until it's parallel to the wind's path. This provides the least resistance and points the arrow in the other direction, *into* the wind.

LET'S GO FLY A KITE!

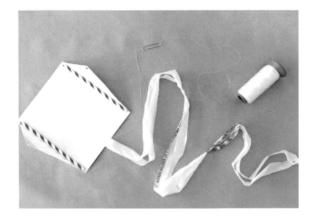

Learn about the fundamentals of flying with this classic "sled" kite.

TIME: 1 HOUR

Fig. 5: You made your very own kite. Now, take it outside to see how high can you fly it!

TOOLS & MATERIALS

- ⊘ standard printer or colored paper
- ⊘ scissors
- ⊘ 2 drinking straws
- ⊘ cellophane tape
- ⊘ masking tape
- ⊘ single-hole punch
- ⊘ kite string
- ⊘ ruler or measuring tape
- ⊘ paper clip
- ⊘ plastic grocery bag
- ⊘ art supplies (optional)

SAFETY TIPS, HINTS & TRICKS

- ⊘ Use a standard-sized piece of paper for your kite: 8½-by-11-inch and A4 sizes both work well.
- ⊘ If you don't have kite string, any other thin, lightweight string or twine will do.
- ⊘ You can recycle any thin plastic bag to make the loops for the tail.

PROTOCOL

STEP 1: To make the base for your kite, cut a piece of standard-sized paper into the shape shown. Decorate it if you want. When you're finished, fold up the triangular side flaps. (Fig. 1)

STEP 2: Lay a straw on each fold of the side flaps and use cellophane tape to secure them in place. (Fig. 2)

STEP 3: Reinforce the points of the flaps with masking tape. Punch a hole in each one.

STEP 4: Cut two 16-inch (40 cm) lengths of string. Tie one end of one piece tightly

Fig. 1: Cut a piece of paper into this six-sided shape and fold up the flaps.

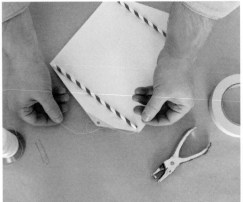

Fig. 2: Tape two straws into place on the folds of the side flaps.

Fig. 3: Tie the strings to your kite.

Fig. 4: Join the rings of plastic bag to make a tail.

through one hole in a side flap. Do the same for the other piece. Tie the remaining ends together on one end of a paper clip and tie the spool of kite string to the other end. (Fig. 3)

STEP 5: Flatten the plastic bag and cut straight across it, making 1-inch (2 cm) strips. Open each strip into a loop. Pull the rings of plastic through one another to link them together and make a tail that is 4 to 5 feet (1.2 to 1.5 m) long. (Fig. 4)

STEP 6: To complete your kite, secure the tail to the bottom center with tape. (Fig. 5)

STEP 7: Take your kite outside. Start by walking with it and then slowly break into a run. What do you observe? Do you feel tugging or tension on the string? How does this change based on the speed that you move?

CREATIVE ENRICHMENT: TAKING IT FURTHER

1. How does the length of your kite's tail affect the way it flies? What is too short or too long? What is the sweet spot in terms of length?

2. Increase the number of tails on your kite, being sure to center and space them evenly. How does the kite fly with two tails versus one, or no tails at all?

THE SCIENCE BEHIND THE FUN

A kite flies because wind creates high pressure against the wide surface of the paper. This causes *lift* perpendicular to the moving air, which pushes it upward. The faster the wind (or the faster you move), the greater the lift.

At the same time, the force of drag pulls the kite in the direction of the wind. Lift and drag work together against the string and gravity to keep the kite aloft.

Attaching a tail to a kite adds weight and increases drag, keeping the kite's bottom down and preventing rolling and spinning. A small tail barely helps, but a tail that's too long makes the kite too heavy to fly. Professional kite makers suggest adding a tail that is three to eight times the length of the kite.

PAPER AIRPLANES

All you need is paper and wind to learn all about how airplanes fly.

TIME: 15 MINUTES

Fig. 5: Grip the body of the plane between your thumb and fingers and let it fly!

TOOLS & MATERIALS

- ⊙ standard printer, notebook, or colored craft paper
- ⊙ tape

SAFETY TIPS, HINTS & TRICKS

- ⊙ Magazine pages also work quite well for this lab and add a bit of color and pattern to your paper airplanes.

PROTOCOL

STEP 1: Fold a piece of paper in half lengthwise. Open the fold and lay the paper flat.

STEP 2: Fold the upper right and upper left corners down until the top edge of the paper lines up with the center fold. (Fig. 1)

STEP 3: Now fold the slanted edges of the "roof" down toward the center fold. Firmly press the folds. (Fig. 2)

STEP 4: To make the wings, fold the triangle in half and then fold the slanted edges back toward the center fold. Again, firmly press all the folds. (Fig. 3)

Fig. 1: Your folded paper should be in the shape of a house with a pointy roof.

Fig. 2: Your folded paper should now look like a large isosceles triangle.

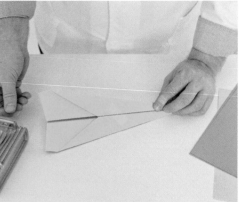

Fig. 3: Form the wings and body by folding the slanted edges back.

Fig. 4: Make the body of the plane, fold out the wings, and tack them in place with tape.

Fig. 6: Turn the back ends of the wings up or down or one of each.

STEP 5: Bend the paper back along the folds to define the body (the part that you grip and use to throw). Bring the wings up and secure them together with a small piece of tape across the folds. (Fig. 4)

STEP 6: Test out your plane: Throw it and let it glide. Notice how it travels. (Fig. 5)

STEP 7: Now, turn up the back ends of each wing slightly, as shown, and throw your airplane again. What do you observe? Turn both back ends down or turn one up and one down. What changes do you observe in the flight pattern? (Fig. 6)

CREATIVE ENRICHMENT: PAPER & PRESSURE MINI LAB

1. Fold a piece of paper in half and hold it at the fold with the edges hanging downward. Blow between the two hanging edges. What do you notice?

2. Tape the ends of a strip of paper together into a teardrop-shaped loop—like the cross-section of an airplane wing, or *airfoil*. Thread a pencil through the loop and blow into the curved surface. What happens?

THE SCIENCE BEHIND THE FUN

Turning up the back ends of the wings of your paper airplane creates pressure that makes it nose upward. Your plane may "stall" and fall to the ground or complete an "inside loop" in midair. When the back ends are turned down, the plane noses down and hits the ground or lands on its back. When the back ends are alternated, the plane spins in a "snap roll."

According to Bernoulli's Principle, a material that flows exerts its lowest pressure wherever it moves the fastest. So, in the mini lab when you blow between the hanging folds of paper, the moving air causes low pressure, and higher-pressure air pushes the folds together.

When in flight, a real airplane wing is positioned so air hits the bottom, creating high pressure. On the upper side, the air speeds up as it's forced between the curve of the wing and the air right above it, creating low pressure. The higher pressure underneath lifts the plane into the air.

Lab 29

WIND EROSION EXPERIMENT

TOOLS & MATERIALS

- safety goggles
- 3 small metal or glass baking pans
- sand
- water
- sponge
- small stones
- hairdryer
- protractor
- stopwatch
- ruler

SAFETY TIPS, HINTS & TRICKS

- This lab can be a little messy because of the sand flying around. It's best to do it outdoors or in a garage or basement that can be swept up afterward.
- Always use a hair dryer under adult supervision.
- Wear your safety goggles at all times to protect your eyes from flying particles of sand.

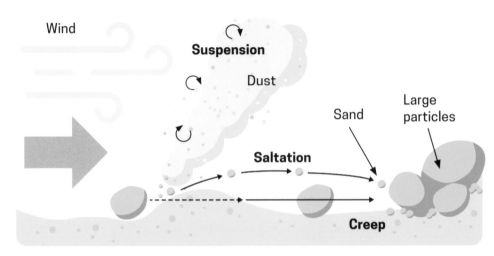

This diagram shows how the wind works to move and shape the land.

Model wind erosion with sand and a hairdryer.

TIME: 30 MINUTES

PROTOCOL

STEP 1: Prepare three pans of sand: (1) dry sand only, (2) a mix of dry sand and small stones, and (3) wet sand. (Fig. 1)

STEP 2: Point the hairdryer at the first pan of sand at a 45-degree angle. Confirm the angle with the protractor. Turn the hairdryer on low for 30 seconds. What do you observe? (Fig. 2)

STEP 3: Do the same thing for the other two pans. What happens for each? Write down what you observe.

Fig. 1: To wet the sand, squeeze water out of a sponge over the surface until it's saturated.

Fig. 2: Point the hairdryer at an angle at the pan of sand for 30 seconds.

Fig. 3: Experiment with the angle of the hairdryer as well as its distance from each pan.

STEP 4: Smooth out the sand in each pan and position the hairdryer in the same place and at the same angle, but this time turn it on high. What do you observe now?

STEP 5: Try the same setup again, but this time use the protractor to make the angle smaller. What differences do you notice in the erosion patterns of the different pans of sand?

STEP 6: Measure a consistent chosen distance from the edge of each pan and repeat the experiment with both different angles and different air speeds. Record your observations. (Fig. 3)

CREATIVE ENRICHMENT: EROSION PREVENTION MINI LAB

Make a small pile of sand and measure its height. Blow air from the hair dryer onto the pile for 30 seconds. Measure its height again. Rebuild the pile, but add materials such as sticks, bits of aluminum foil, or gravel. Test the hairdryer at different speeds, distances, and angles, rebuilding the pile each time and measuring its before and after heights. What materials are best at slowing erosion, and why?

THE SCIENCE BEHIND THE FUN

For loose sand, winds as slow as 13 miles per hour (21 kph) can start to move the soil, and that movement increases with wind speed. The rate of erosion caused by a 30-mile-per-hour (48-kph) wind is more than three times that of a 20-mile-per-hour (32 kph) wind.

Wind blows dry sand away quickly because the individual grains don't stick to one another. In wet sand, water fills in the spaces between the grains and surface tension holds them together, so it takes more effort to blow the sand away. Wind erosion decreases as soil moisture increases.

The erosion of surface soil is a real threat to agriculture because it makes the land less productive by removing its most fertile parts. The best way to prevent this is by planting trees around crop fields or growing crops that hold the soil and keep winds off the surface.

Lab 30

AIR POLLUTION SENSOR

TOOLS & MATERIALS

- ⟩ piece of clear plastic
- ⟩ scissors
- ⟩ packing tape
- ⟩ clean wood block, brick, or similar weighted object
- ⟩ petroleum jelly
- ⟩ small paintbrush
- ⟩ blank white paper
- ⟩ magnifying glass
- ⟩ smartphone or high-resolution digital camera (optional)

SAFETY TIPS, HINTS & TRICKS

- ⟩ For the piece of clear plastic, you can use transparency acetate, a clear sheet protector, or even a zip-top bag. If you use cling wrap, layer a couple of pieces together before cutting to size.
- ⟩ You can use either a brush or your finger to apply the petroleum jelly to the plastic.

Petroleum jelly and a piece of plastic are all you need to measure particle pollution in the air.

TIME: 2 DAYS

Fig. 4: All sorts of small particles become lodged in the petroleum jelly.

PROTOCOL

STEP 1: Cut the piece of plastic to fit your wood block or weighted object and secure it in place using packing tape along the edges. (Fig. 1)

STEP 2: Coat the top surface of the plastic with a ¹⁄₁₆-inch (1.5 mm) thick layer of petroleum jelly using the paintbrush. (Fig. 2)

STEP 3: Choose an open, outdoor location with good air circulation. Place your sensor upright on an elevated, level surface where it will be safe and secure.

STEP 4: Let the sensor sit in the same place for at least 24 hours, weather permitting.

STEP 5: Collect the piece of plastic, remove it from the wood block or brick, and place it on a sheet of white paper. Examine your sensor. Use your magnifying glass to look closely at the particles of matter in the petroleum jelly. What do you see? (Fig. 3)

STEP 6: Take a close-up, high-resolution photo of your sensor. Zoom in on the photo. What do you see now? (Fig. 4)

Fig. 1: Trim the plastic to size and attach it to a weighted object with tape.

Fig. 2: Paint a thin layer of petroleum jelly on to the piece of plastic.

Fig. 3: Put the plastic on white paper and look at it through a magnifier.

CREATIVE ENRICHMENT: TAKING IT FURTHER

1. Make two sensors and place them in different locations, such as school and home or indoors and outdoors. Compare the pollution collected by each.

2. Put out a sensor every three months in the same spot. Do you notice seasonal changes in the kinds of particles in the air?

THE SCIENCE BEHIND THE FUN

Particle pollution, or particulate matter, is tiny pieces of solid or liquid suspended in the air. In this lab, you made a very simple tool to catch and observe particles such as dust, dirt, pollen, and ash.

Particulate matter comes from primary sources, such as wood stoves or forest fires, as well as secondary sources, such as power plants and coal fires, that emit gases that form particles once they're in the air. Other sources include factories, cars and trucks, construction sites, and plants and trees.

Breathing in particle pollution can be harmful to your health. Coarse particles, such as dust and pollen, can irritate your eyes, nose, and throat. Fine particles, such as asbestos and coal dust, can get deeper into the lungs and cause more serious health problems.

UNIT 5
SEVERE WEATHER EVENTS

Compared to other planets in our solar system, Earth has generally mild weather, but occasionally, severe weather events unleash incredible fury on our planet's surface.

Thunderstorms grow quickly as huge, anvil-shaped clouds flatten out at the tropopause—where the troposphere meets the stratosphere. They fill the sky with great sparks of lightning that burn the air and produce booming thunder.

Hailstones form in these clouds as strong updrafts keep frozen water droplets suspended in the air. Spherical chunks of ice can grow to the size of golf balls or even larger before falling to the ground. And vortexes of fast-spinning air extend down to the ground as tornadoes, bringing destruction as they go.

Hurricanes form over tropical oceans when huge masses of warm, moist air rise and begin to spin. These superstorms bring damaging winds, tons of rain, and huge storm surges to coastal communities. All of that water floods rivers, streams, and lakes and causes mudslides that change the shape of the land.

In the desert, high winds whip up dust and sand into huge surface-level clouds, making it difficult to breathe and see. Dust from these storms can get high into the atmosphere and travel thousands of miles before falling back to Earth.

In this unit's labs, you'll use homemade devices to safely model and study each of these natural events, which are far too dangerous to experience in person. We'll leave that to the meteorologists and storm chasers!

BUILD A THUNDER TUBE

TOOLS & MATERIALS

- ⊙ large cardboard oatmeal container, approx. 5" diameter × 9½" tall (13 × 24 cm)
- ⊙ tape
- ⊙ small nail
- ⊙ screen door spring, approx. ½" diameter x 6" long (1.3 x 15 cm)
- ⊙ pliers
- ⊙ measuring tape
- ⊙ wire cutters
- ⊙ glue
- ⊙ crayons, markers, and other art supplies (optional)

SAFETY TIPS, HINTS & TRICKS

- ⊙ Make sure your container has a cardboard bottom. Metal or plastic bottoms do not work as well.
- ⊙ You'll want an adult's assistance while using the nail and when stretching and cutting the spring, which requires a bit of force.

Make thunder without lightning with this DIY musical instrument made from an oatmeal container and a spring.

TIME: 1 HOUR

Fig. 5: The cardboard container amplifies the sound of the spring.

PROTOCOL

STEP 1: Peel off the oatmeal label. Wrap the container in craft paper, if desired, and decorate it as you like.

STEP 2: Reinforce the center of the bottom of the container with a piece of tape. Ask an adult to help you use a small nail to punch a small hole through the tape into the container. (Fig. 1)

STEP 3: Leave a few coils compressed at one end of the spring and stretch out the rest of the spring so about ½ inch (1.3 cm) of space remains between each of the coils. (Fig. 2)

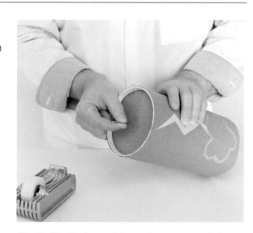

Fig. 1: Push the nail into the center of the container's bottom.

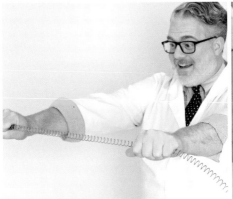

Fig. 2: Stretch the spring so there is permanent space between the coils.

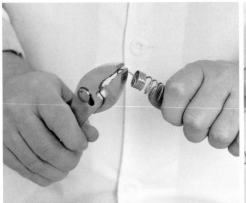

Fig. 3: Trim the spring and make a hook on the other end.

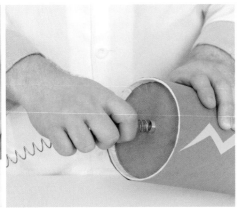

Fig. 4: Secure the spring to the bottom with glue once it's been twisted into the hole.

STEP 4: Have an adult use wire cutters to cut the spring to about 36 inches (91 cm) long and use pliers to bend up a hook from the last bit of wire on the compressed end. (Fig. 3)

STEP 5: Pass this hook through the hole in the bottom of the container and turn the spring about three times until it is threaded onto the cardboard. Apply a small dab of glue near the hole to secure the spring in place. (Fig. 4)

STEP 6: Shake your new contraption to make the sound of thunder. (Fig. 5)

CREATIVE ENRICHMENT: LIGHTNING DISTANCE MINI LAB

Light travels much faster than sound. You see lightning immediately, but it can take a bit of time to hear thunder. Because of this you can find the distance between you and a lightning strike.

Simply count the number of seconds between a flash of lightning and the sound of thunder (or use a stopwatch). Multiply this number by 1,129 feet per second (344 m/s)—the speed of sound. Divide your answer by 5,280 to learn how many miles away the lightning is (use 1,000 for kilometers).

Example:

$$
\begin{array}{rl}
& 7 \text{ seconds} \\
\times & 1{,}129 \text{ feet/second} \\
\div & 5{,}280 \text{ feet/mile} \\
\hline
& 1.5 \text{ miles (away)}
\end{array}
$$

THE SCIENCE BEHIND THE FUN

When lightning strikes, it can deliver an electrical force of 1 billion volts and up to 200,000 amps of electricity. This intense energy heats the air, which rapidly expands to produce a sonic shock wave you hear as thunder.

Lightning can travel many miles through the air before it strikes the ground. When you listen to thunder, you first hear the sound created by the part of the lightning closest to you, followed by the sound of the parts further away. A sharp crack tells you that lightning passed nearby, whereas a rumble means it was several miles away.

LIGHTNING AT HOME

TOOLS & MATERIALS

- ⊘ latex balloon
- ⊘ piece of wool or fur
- ⊘ fluorescent (tube) light bulb
- ⊘ aluminum pie pan
- ⊘ piece of styrofoam
- ⊘ unsharpened pencil with a new eraser
- ⊘ thumbtack

This collection of experiments explores the wonders of static electricity and lightning.

TIME: 30 MINUTES

A bolt of lightning can superheat the air around it to 50,000°F (27,760°C)— about four times the temperature of the surface of the sun.

SAFETY TIPS, HINTS & TRICKS

- ⊘ This lab works best in dry air. It will work somewhat all year-round, but the air inside most homes has the lowest humidity during the winter.
- ⊘ Please handle the fluorescent light bulb with care.

PROTOCOL

STEP 1: Blow up the balloon and tie it off. Rub it rapidly with the wool or fur (or on your hair). What do you notice? Hold the balloon close to your face. What do you feel? (Fig. 1)

Fig. 1: Charge a balloon by rubbing it on your head.

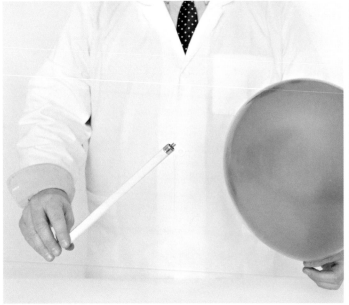

Fig. 2: Use the charged balloon to make a fluorescent bulb glow.

Fig. 3: Make a handle for the pie pan with a pencil and a thumbtack.

STEP 2: Rub the balloon again. Place the balloon against a wall and let it go. What happens, and why?

STEP 3: Turn off the lights in the room and rub the balloon as before for several seconds. Hold the charged balloon near the end of the fluorescent light bulb. What do you observe? How can you build up a bigger charge to get the bulb to glow brighter? (Fig. 2)

STEP 4: Push the thumbtack through the center of the pie pan from the bottom and press the eraser end of the pencil into the thumbtack. (Fig. 3)

STEP 5: Place the piece of styrofoam on a table and rub it vigorously with the wool or fur.

CONTINUED

CREATIVE ENRICHMENT: LIGHTNING IN YOUR MOUTH MINI LAB

Stand in front of a mirror in a really dark room. While keeping your lips open, break up a wintergreen hard candy between your teeth. What do you observe?

The science: crushing sugar molecules releases electrons that excite nitrogen molecules in the air, causing them to emit UV light. The wintergreen flavoring, methyl salicylate (MEH-thl sa-luh-SILL-ate), absorbs this radiation and emits it as blue light—a phenomenon known as triboluminescence (TRY-bo-lu-muh-NESS-uhnts).

Fig. 4: Transfer the charge from the styrofoam to the pie pan and touch it to feel a spark.

STEP 6: Pick up the aluminum pie pan using the pencil as a handle and place it on top of the styrofoam. Touch the pie pan with your finger. What do you feel? Do you hear anything? (Fig. 4)

STEP 7: Repeat Steps 2 and 3, but before you touch the pie pan again, turn off the lights and make the room as dark as possible. What do you see when you touch the pan?

THE SCIENCE BEHIND THE FUN

When you rub a balloon with wool or fur or your hair, electrons are transferred to it, giving it a negative charge. This charge repels electrons on other surfaces, making them positively charged, and causes the balloon to stick. Holding the charged balloon near a fluorescent light excites mercury atoms inside the bulb, which emit UV light that causes phosphors in the tube to glow.

Inside a thundercloud, millions of bits of ice bump into each other as they swirl through the air. These collisions build up a charge in the cloud, which is released as a giant spark of lightning in the clouds or between the clouds and the ground.

As with the balloon, rubbing styrofoam with wool or fur also gives it a negative charge. This is carefully transferred to the aluminum pie pan, and when you touch it, electricity flows through your body down to the positively charged ground. The resulting spark is a mini bolt of lightning!

HURRICANE FIDGET SPINNER

Build a version of this popular toy using everyday materials, such as cardboard and coins, to model a spinning hurricane.

TIME: 45 MINUTES

Fig. 6: It's time to play with your hurricane fidget spinner!

TOOLS & MATERIALS

- thick cardboard
- drawing compass
- scissors or craft knife
- art supplies (markers, glitter, paint, and stickers)
- 4 small coins, ½" to ¾" (1 to 2 cm) in diameter
- hot glue gun and hot glue sticks
- pushpin
- round toothpick or bamboo skewer
- coffee stirrer straw
- thin cardboard

SAFETY TIPS, HINTS & TRICKS

- Use caution when handling sharp tools, such as scissors, the knife, or the compass.
- Symmetry and balance are important for the shape and weight of your spinner to make sure it spins freely without listing to one side or catching on itself.
- Have an adult help with the hot glue as well as drawing and cutting out the spinner and cutting the toothpick.

PROTOCOL

STEP 1: Use the drawing compass to trace a 3½-inch (9 cm) circle on the thick cardboard. Cut this circle out with the scissors or craft knife.

STEP 2: Use a pencil and a ruler to divide the circle into 8 equal sections. All around the edge, draw and cut out a curved notch from each section, creating pointed "arms" to represent the cloud bands of a hurricane. This is the spinner part of your toy. (Fig. 1)

CONTINUED

Fig. 1: Shape a symmetrical saw blade from thick cardboard.

Fig. 2: Embellish your spinner. Make it look like a hurricane!

Fig. 3: Give your spinner some weight with coins. Glue them near the edges, outside the center circle.

STEP 3: Draw a 1-inch (2.5 cm) circle in the middle of both sides of the spinner. Decorate one side with your favorite art supplies, being sure to stay outside the center circle you drew. (Fig. 2)

STEP 4: On the opposite side of the spinner, use hot glue to attach four small coins in a square formation, equally spaced, as close to the edge as possible without being visible from the other side. (Fig. 3)

STEP 5: Use the pushpin to poke a hole in the center of the spinner. Widen the hole with the toothpick or skewer until it's the same diameter as the coffee stirrer straw.

STEP 6: Insert the straw through the hole, perpendicular to the spinner. Use small dabs of hot glue to hold it in place on both sides. Once the glue has set, trim the straw to about ⅛ inch (3 mm) on either side. (Fig. 4)

STEP 7: Draw and cut out two 1-inch (2.5 cm) circles from thin cardboard. Make a hole in the exact center of each with the pushpin.

STEP 8: Thread the spinning disc onto the toothpick. Thread a small cardboard circle onto each end and sandwich the spinner between them. Allow a tiny bit of space (approx. $1/16$ inch [1.5 mm]) between each circle and the coffee stirrer straw. The disk should spin freely.

STEP 9: Use a few dabs of hot glue to secure each circle in place and use scissors to trim the toothpick ends. (Fig. 5)

STEP 10: Once the glue has set, hold the smaller cardboard discs between your thumb and your middle finger and use your index finger to make the hurricane spin. (Fig. 6)

TIP: Hurricanes spin counter-clockwise in the Northern Hemisphere and clockwise in the Southern Hemisphere.

Fig. 4: Hot glue a coffee stirrer straw into the center of your spinner and trim it to size.

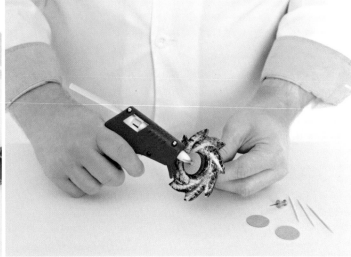

Fig. 5: Hot glue the circles to the toothpick and trim the ends.

CREATIVE ENRICHMENT: HURRICANE IN A BOWL MINI LAB

Fill a large glass bowl with warm water. Use a mixing spoon to stir the water and get it moving. Add a few drops of blue food coloring to the center. Watch it swirl and move out into the bowl. Squirt a bit of shaving cream into the bowl as clouds. How does this resemble a hurricane?

THE SCIENCE BEHIND THE FUN

Hurricanes (also called typhoons or tropical cyclones) form over the warm ocean waters near the equator. They are defined by their spinning action, spiraling bands of clouds, and very distinct center "eye."

Hot, humid air from the surface flows upward, creating an area of low pressure. Air from surrounding areas with higher air pressure pushes its way in. That air also becomes warm and moist and also rises. This continues to happen, with the surrounding air swirling in to take the place of warm, rising air.

Higher in the atmosphere, the warmed air begins to cool and water condenses, creating bands of cumulonimbus clouds that make up the storm. The whole system of clouds and wind begins to spin, fed by the ocean's heat and water evaporating from its surface.

MODEL HAIL FORMATION

TOOLS & MATERIALS

- ping-pong balls
- hair dryer
- paper towel or toilet paper tube
- latex balloon
- small coin

SAFETY TIPS, HINTS & TRICKS

- The diameter of the cardboard tube should be slightly larger than the ping-pong ball.
- Always use a hair dryer under adult supervision.

Use a hair dryer and ping-pong balls to model how hail is formed.

TIME: 15 MINUTES

Fig. 1: Balance a ping-pong ball in the jet of air coming out of a hair dryer.

PROTOCOL

STEP 1: Switch on the hair dryer to "cool" and point it upward.

STEP 2: Hold a ping-pong ball above the hair dryer and try to balance it in the stream of air so that it stays up without you holding it. Try both the high and low settings. What do you observe? Which setting works best? (Fig. 1)

STEP 3: See how far you can tilt the hair dryer to the side before the ping-pong ball falls. (Fig. 2)

STEP 4: Hold the cardboard tube vertically, right over the ball. What happens, and why? (Fig. 3)

Fig. 2: How far can you tilt the hair dryer and still hold on to the ball?

Fig. 3: See what happens when you hold a cardboard tube over the ball.

Fig. 4: Try to float two ping pong balls in the air stream with the hair dryer set on high.

Fig. 5: Float a balloon over the ping-pong ball.

STEP 5: Finally, test the strength of your hair dryer's jet of air. Try to balance more than one ping-pong ball. What change in their behavior do you observe? (Fig. 4)

CREATIVE ENRICHMENT: TAKING IT FURTHER

1. Push a small coin through the neck of a latex balloon to add a little weight and then inflate it to a 7-inch (18 cm) diameter. Place it over the ping-pong ball. What do you notice? (Fig. 5)

2. With assistance from an adult, use the stream of water from a garden hose or a leaf blower in place of the hair dryer. Float larger and heavier objects, such as tennis balls, softballs, or beachballs, in the air or water flow. Which objects stay in which stream the best, and why?

THE SCIENCE BEHIND THE FUN

The stream of air coming out of a hair dryer moves very fast and, as you learned in Lab 28, Bernoulli's Principle says that a material that flows exerts its lowest pressure wherever it moves the fastest. This means the air from the hair dryer has lower pressure than the air around it. The ping-pong ball stays in this moving column as the surrounding high-pressure air pushes equally on all sides of it. Gravity pulls the ball down as the air forces it up. The ball hovers when all the forces are balanced.

When you place the paper tube above the ping-pong ball, the air is funneled into a smaller area, making it move faster. The pressure in the tube falls, and the ball is quickly pushed up inside and through, shooting into the air.

During very strong thunderstorms, frozen droplets of water fall from the clouds but are pushed back up by strong updrafts—just like your ping-pong balls and the hair dryer. They encounter other water droplets that freeze around them in a layer of ice. This starts the formation of hailstones, which rise and fall many times, growing in size until they're too heavy to be kept aloft and so they fall to the ground.

TORNADO IN A BOTTLE

Lab 35

TOOLS & MATERIALS

- ⊘ two 2-liter plastic bottles
- ⊘ funnel
- ⊘ water
- ⊘ metal washer
- ⊘ hot glue gun and hot glue sticks
- ⊘ electrical tape
- ⊘ duct tape or other heavy-duty tape
- ⊘ small plastic beads (optional)
- ⊘ lamp oil (optional)

SAFETY TIPS, HINTS & TRICKS

- ⊘ The metal washer should be the same diameter as the mouth of the plastic bottles, about 1 inch (2.5 cm). The hole in the center can be on the larger side, about ½" (1.3 cm).
- ⊘ If you use plastic beads, make sure they fit easily through the hole in the washer.
- ⊘ Lamp oil floats on water and helps to color your tornado so it is more visible.
- ⊘ Ask an adult to help you with the hot glue.

With two plastic bottles and some water, build a toy that models a tornado.

TIME: 30 MINUTES

Fig. 5: Swirl the bottles around to create a whirlpool of air, water, lamp oil, and beads.

PROTOCOL

STEP 1: Using the funnel, fill one bottle about three-quarters of the way with water. If you have them, add a handful of beads and/or ¼ cup (60 ml) of colored lamp oil. (Fig. 1)

STEP 2: Secure a metal washer to the mouth of the bottle with hot glue. (Fig. 2)

STEP 3: Apply hot glue to the mouth of the second bottle and position it upside down over the washer. Use more glue to create a good seal between the bottles. Let the glue set completely. (Fig. 3)

Fig. 1: Add water to one soda bottle along with lamp oil and plastic beads.

Fig. 2: Use a thin bead of hot glue to attach the washer to the bottle.

Fig. 3: Connect the second bottle with hot glue.

Fig. 4: Wrap the bottle necks in electrical tape and finish with duct tape.

STEP 4: Wrap the connection in a layer of electrical tape for an additional seal and a layer of duct tape (or other heavy-duty tape) for strength. (Fig. 4)

STEP 5: Turn your device over and swirl the bottles in a circular motion. What do you observe? If you've added the lamp oil and/or the plastic beads, how do they behave? (Fig. 5)

CREATIVE ENRICHMENT: DID YOU KNOW?

The fastest winds on Earth occur inside tornadoes and are classified based on the Enhanced Fujita (EF) scale, a 0 to 5 rating system that estimates wind speeds based on the damage they do. (Fig. 6)

RATING	WIND SPEED	DAMAGE
EF0	65-85 mph	minor roof, branches
EF1	86-100 mph	broken windows
EF2	111-135 mph	roofs off, large trees
EF3	136-165 mph	homes damaged
EF4	166-200 mph	homes leveled
EF5	200+ mph	incredible damage

THE SCIENCE BEHIND THE FUN

Tornadoes are born inside thunderstorms when very strong winds at high altitudes swirl and roll over the slower air below them. Strong, warm updrafts push on this horizontal cylinder of spinning air and tilt it to vertical. Cold downward drafts push the resulting funnel toward the ground, forming a vortex that lengthens as it pulls up warm air from below. In order to be called a tornado, this vortex must touch the ground, where it can travel for miles and do incredible damage.

Swirling your bottle device in a circular motion causes a vortex inside. This makes it easier for air to flow into the top bottle from the bottom one through the center of the neck, while the water (and oil and beads) flows out by swirling around the edges.

Fig. 6: This scale was introduced in 1971 by Ted Fujita and enhanced for accuracy in 2007.

MODEL A LANDSLIDE

Construct a landslide experiment using recycled cartons and soil.

TOOLS & MATERIALS

- 2 half-gallon (1.89 L) milk or juice cartons
- tape or stapler (optional)
- scissors or craft knife
- sand
- potting soil
- shoebox or similar container
- marker
- water
- spray bottle

TIME: 30 MINUTES

A landslide on a mountain after heavy rain

SAFETY TIPS, HINTS & TRICKS

- Be sure that the cartons you use are very clean.
- Craft knives are sharp and require adult assistance.
- The shoebox or container should be big enough to hold both of the cartons diagonally upright.

PROTOCOL

STEP 1: Keep the spout caps on the cartons, if they have them, or make sure the folded spout flaps at the top are firmly closed with tape or staples. Create two "landslide trays" by cutting one side out of each carton. (Fig. 1)

STEP 2: Fill one tray with 2 inches (5 cm) of soil. Mix in a little bit of water from a spray bottle so it stays in place when you tilt the carton at an angle. Do the same for the second tray and the sand. (Fig. 2)

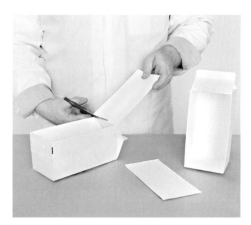

Fig. 1: Cut the cartons to make landslide trays.

Fig. 2: Fill one tray with soil and one with sand. Add a little bit of water for stability.

Fig. 3: Prop up the landslide trays diagonally opposite one another in a shoebox.

Fig. 4: Make a landslide mark in each tray.

STEP 3: Prop one carton up on the long side of the shoebox or container at a steep angle. Position the other carton the same way but on the opposite side of the box so the setup doesn't tip over. (Fig. 3)

STEP 4: Draw a line 1 inch (2.5 cm) below the top of each landslide tray. When the sand or the soil moves below this line, it will count as a landslide. (Fig. 4)

STEP 5: Start spraying water at the top of each tray. Count how many sprays it takes until the material in each tray falls below the line. Which do you think will slide first? (Fig. 5)

CREATIVE ENRICHMENT: TAKING IT FURTHER

1. What kinds of things can you insert into your soil or sand to slow down or prevent the landslide?

2. Weigh your spray bottle before and after the experiment. This will tell you how much water was needed to cause a landslide.

Fig. 5: Spray water on both the sand and the soil until they each fall below the mark.

THE SCIENCE BEHIND THE FUN

While landslides are not weather events themselves, they are often the result of extreme weather that brings a lot of precipitation to one location in a short period of time. They can also reveal how human activity has damaged the natural ability of the land to absorb runoff effectively.

The likelihood of a landslide, big or small, depends on how steep the slope is, the type of soil or sand, and whether there are plants growing in it. Plants absorb water and reduce infiltration—the movement of water from the surface into the ground—that would otherwise weaken soil and cause it to slide.

SANDSTORM TUNNEL

TOOLS & MATERIALS

- ⊘ safety goggles
- ⊘ 2 or 3 large cardboard boxes of the same dimensions
- ⊘ utility knife or box cutter
- ⊘ tape
- ⊘ hair dryer
- ⊘ sand
- ⊘ confectioners' sugar
- ⊘ dustpan and brush or a small broom
- ⊘ black paper or black paint and a paintbrush (optional)

SAFETY TIPS, HINTS & TRICKS

- ⊘ This is a rather large and messy setup and it is best to do it with adult assistance and outside or in a garage or basement, where you can easily sweep up afterward.
- ⊘ Utility knives and box cutters are very sharp. Please have an adult help with the cutting portion of this lab.
- ⊘ Wear your safety goggles at all times to protect your eyes from flying particles of sand and sugar.

Experiment with sand, confectioners' sugar, and a hair dryer to see how sandstorms form.

TIME: 2 HOURS

The spectacular front of a sandstorm churning through Khartoum, Sudan.

PROTOCOL

STEP 1: Tape the boxes together in a long rectangular tube, 5 to 8 feet long (1.5 to 2.4 m). One end should be open and the other should be closed. Use the utility knife or box cutter to cut off the top of the tube so that you can see into the "wind tunnel" you've created. (Fig. 1)

STEP 2: This step is optional, but to make it easier to see the dust storm you'll be creating, you can line the tunnel in black paper or paint it with black paint. (Fig. 2)

STEP 3: Place a small sand pile at the tunnel's opening. Turn the hair dryer on high and point it at the sand. How did the sand behave? How far did it travel? (Fig. 3)

Fig. 1: Use boxes to make a long cardboard wind tunnel with an open top.

Fig. 2: A black tunnel makes it easier to see the experiment.

Fig. 3: Direct the stream of air from a hair dryer onto the pile of sand.

Fig. 4: Make a more noticeable dust cloud with the two materials mixed together.

STEP 4: Clean up the wind tunnel and try the same thing with the confectioners' sugar. What do you observe? Was there a dust cloud?

STEP 5: Make a 1 to 1 mixture of sand and sugar and place a pile at the opening of the wind tunnel. Turn on the hair dryer as before and watch what happens. Did you create a dust storm? Why and how? (Fig. 4)

CREATIVE ENRICHMENT: SANDSTORM IN A BOTTLE MINI LAB

Pour about 1 ounce (30 ml) of clear glue into a recycled, clear, 16 to 20 ounce (473 to 591 ml) plastic water bottle and fill it three-quarters full with warm water. Cap the bottle and shake it until thoroughly mixed. Add 1 to 2 tablespoons (15 to 30 ml) of water-soluble gold metallic or pearlescent paint to the solution and top it off with more water. Screw the cap on tightly and shake and spin your bottle to see your sandstorm work!

THE SCIENCE BEHIND THE FUN

Sandstorms can be triggered by sudden rain in a very dry area. Raindrops fall, but it's so hot and dry that they evaporate before hitting the ground. This cools the air, which becomes denser and falls very quickly. When this air hits the ground, it bounces back up, carrying dust particles with it.

Sand grains are round and get lifted up by wind like airplane wings. They leap off the surface into the air in a process known as *saltation*. These sand particles hit the surface and loosen other particles, which are lifted into the atmosphere and transported long distances via *suspension* (as shown in the diagram on page 82).

In this experiment, there's not enough force to keep the sand suspended, so the moving air from the hair dryer picks it up and quickly deposits it a short distance away. The confectioners' sugar clumps and sticks to itself, resulting in very little blowing dust. But when you mix the two together, the particles of sand slam into the confectioners' sugar, putting very small particles of cornstarch and sugar into the air to be stirred up into a cloud by the hairdryer.

UNIT 6
WHEN IT'S COLD AND SNOWY

On Earth, cold and snowy weather occurs primarily at and near the poles, where snowpack builds up and compresses to form ice caps, ice sheets, and glaciers. It also occurs in the temperate and continental climate zones of both hemispheres during their respective winters.

As you move higher up into the atmosphere, temperatures drop significantly, so cold weather also happens at higher altitudes. The tallest mountains, such as Mount Everest and K2, have snowcaps year-round, and temperatures at their summits are never above freezing.

At night, deserts can experience freezing temperatures too because there is little to no water vapor in the air to trap heat. But, for the very same reason, they rarely, if ever, experience snow.

Don't worry if it's rarely cold and snow doesn't fall where you live. In this unit, there are plenty of opportunities to experiment. You'll start by learning all about the special properties of ice and how water freezes from a liquid into six-sided crystals. Then you'll craft snowflake models from recycled six-pack rings.

You'll make fake snow that looks and feels just like the real thing and model a blizzard inside the jar of a DIY snow globe. You'll mix up a special batch of solution to make bubbles and freeze them right in your kitchen freezer, and you'll end the unit by supercooling water with ice and salt and watching it freeze instantly as you pour it over an ice cube!

BUILD A SNOW GAUGE

Turn a yardstick into a simple tool to measure snowfall.

TIME: 1 HOUR

Fig. 4: Make sure your snow gauge is standing up as straight as possible.

TOOLS & MATERIALS

- ⟩ yardstick or meterstick
- ⟩ bamboo skewers
- ⟩ carpenter's glue
- ⟩ white paint
- ⟩ paintbrush
- ⟩ measuring tape or second yardstick
- ⟩ permanent marker
- ⟩ craft foam sheets
- ⟩ ribbon
- ⟩ scissors
- ⟩ beads, googly eyes, and other craft embellishments
- ⟩ hot glue gun and hot glue sticks

SAFETY TIPS, HINTS & TRICKS

- ⟩ Get an adult to help you glue the skewers to the yardstick and push the gauge into the ground.
- ⟩ As always, use caution when working with hot glue.

PROTOCOL

STEP 1: Position two bamboo skewers on the back of a yardstick along the edges, extending about 4 inches (10 cm) past the end. Attach each one with a bead of carpenter's glue. Allow it to dry. (Fig. 1)

STEP 2: Paint the entire thing, using as many coats as necessary—at least two—to cover the wood and any writing. Let this dry completely.

STEP 3: Use the measuring tape or extra yardstick to mark 1-inch (or 1 cm) measurements along the entire gauge with a permanent marker. Label every mark with its respective number. (Fig.2)

STEP 4: Cut out all the shapes you need for a snowman from the craft foam: body, arms, nose, and hat. Use a piece of ribbon as a scarf, googly eyes for the face, and choose beads for the mouth and buttons. Using hot glue, build your snowman and attach it to the top of the gauge. (Fig. 3)

Fig. 1: Attach the skewers to the end of the yardstick with carpenter's glue.

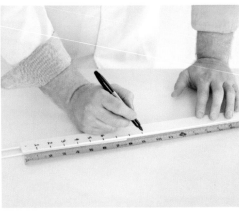

Fig. 2: Mark and label the measurement marks on the painted stick.

Fig. 3: Build a snowman with craft supplies and a hot glue gun.

STEP 5: Choose an open, level area. Insert the skewers straight into the ground so that the bottom of the gauge is flush with the surface. (Fig. 4)

STEP 6: When it snows, measure the total snowfall from the storm, or use beginning and ending measurements over several hours to measure the rate of snowfall.

CREATIVE ENRICHMENT: SNOW OBSERVATION MINI LAB

To get more accurate values, make two or three gauges and place them in different locations. Take an average of their measurements. What factors might cause their differences?

THE SCIENCE BEHIND THE FUN

Meteorologists also use gauges to measure snowfall, but their equipment is a bit more advanced than a yardstick. Scientific snow gauges consist of two parts: a funnel gauge at the top that catches the snow and a copper container below that holds it.

After snow is collected, the container is removed and replaced with a new one. The snow is then melted right in the container and poured into a glass graduated cylinder. Because snow can take up a different amount of space depending on how wet or dense it is, melting it into liquid water allows for a more accurate measurement. While the depth of snow is normally measured in centimeters, melted snow is reported in milliliters.

WHAT'S IN SNOW?

TOOLS & MATERIALS

- 3 or 4 plastic collection containers
- snow
- measuring cups
- permanent marker
- masking tape
- coffee filters
- funnel
- quart-size jar or bottle
- wax paper
- baking sheet
- magnifying glass
- microwave (optional)

SAFETY TIPS, HINTS & TRICKS

- To collect snow for this experiment, you can use quart-size food containers, recycled soda bottles with their tops cut off, or anything similar.
- When using a heat source such as a microwave, make sure you ask an adult for help.

Filter melted snow through a coffee filter to learn about pollution in frozen precipitation.

TIME: 30 MINUTES

Freshly fallen snow appears clean and white but can contain billions of tiny particles of dust and other pollution.

PROTOCOL

STEP 1: Collect samples of snow from different areas near where you live. Use a measuring cup to get the same amount of snow from each location. (Fig. 1)

STEP 2: With masking tape and a marker, label each container with the collection location and bring the containers inside. (Fig. 2)

STEP 3: Let the snow melt completely at room temperature or speed up the process by putting each container in the microwave for 30 seconds at a time. If you do this, make sure your containers are microwave safe. (Fig. 3)

Fig. 1: Collect samples of snow using a measuring cup.

Fig. 2: Label your snow samples.

Fig. 3: Melt each sample of snow just until it turns to water.

Fig. 4: Set up the filtering apparatus with a funnel and a labeled coffee filter.

STEP 4: Grab a coffee filter for each of your samples. Label each filter on the edge in permanent marker with the location where you collected the snow sample.

STEP 5: Place the funnel in the jar or bottle and place one of the coffee filters in the funnel. (Fig. 4)

STEP 6: Pour the water from each snow sample through its matching coffee filter. Make sure you get as much of your sample out of the container as possible.

STEP 7: Once all of the liquid passes through it, remove the filter and lay it face up on a piece of wax paper on the baking sheet. Do this for all your samples.

STEP 8: Let the filters dry undisturbed. Then, observe each one with a magnifying glass. What do you see? Which samples yielded more pollution than others?

CREATIVE ENRICHMENT: TAKING IT FURTHER

1. Use the pH indicator paper you made with cabbage juice in Lab 22 (page 66) to test the pH of the water from each of your snow samples. What do you discover?

2. How can you see whether there are salts dissolved in your sample? Reference Lab 13 (page 44) for a couple of ideas.

THE SCIENCE BEHIND THE FUN

Every snowflake starts as tiny ice crystals forming around a very small piece of dust or dirt. This process, called *deposition*, occurs when supercooled water vapor in clouds *deposits* as ice crystals on particles floating in the air, skipping the liquid phase of matter.

Acid snow is the frozen version of acid rain. Both are polluted by sulfur dioxide and nitrogen oxide gas from burning fossil fuels. You may also find salt in one or more of your samples because it's used to melt ice and snow in the winter and is often applied to roads, sidewalks, and stairs before a storm.

RECYCLED SNOWFLAKES

TOOLS & MATERIALS

- 12 six-pack rings for each snowflake
- cellophane tape or stapler
- string or twine
- scissors

SAFETY TIPS, HINTS & TRICKS

- Collect your family's six-pack rings and keep them out of a landfill.
- You might need the help of an adult to pull the string taught and to tie a secure knot.

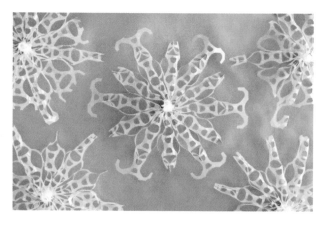

Use six-pack rings to make larger-than-life snowflake models.

TIME: 30 MINUTES

Fig. 6: Trim the end of every other folded six-pack ring "arm" to get a six-sided snowflake.

PROTOCOL

STEP 1: Fold each set of six-pack rings in half lengthwise. Tape the top and bottom sections together in the center of the outer edge of each of the outer rings. (Fig. 1)

STEP 2: Connect the twelve sets side by side, taping adjacent sets at the middle of the edge of the center rings. (Fig. 2)

STEP 3: Thread a piece of string or twine through the bottom rings. Cinch and tie them together tightly with a secure knot. (Fig. 3)

Fig. 2: Use tape to connect all twelve of the folded six-pack rings by their middle rings.

Fig. 1: Fold the six-pack rings in half and secure with pieces of tape on each end.

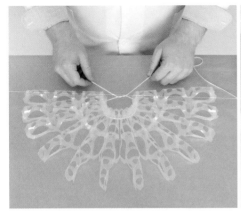

Fig. 3: Gather the bottom rings with a piece of twine to form the middle of the snowflake.

Fig. 4: Use a piece of tape to complete the ring.

Fig. 5: Weave string through the center small loops and pull tight to flatten the snowflake and make it hold its shape.

STEP 4: Attach the center of the outer edge of the first set of rings with the center of the outer edge of the last set of rings, as in Step 2, to complete the shape. (Fig. 4)

STEP 5: Thread another piece of string through each of the small loops at the center of the snowflake. Cinch and tie them together tightly with a secure knot. (Fig. 5)

STEP 6: To finish your snowflake, cut the ends off every other set of six-pack rings, in the desired configuration. You can hang your snowflake with string or twine. (Fig. 6)

CREATIVE ENRICHMENT: SNOW OBSERVATION MINI LAB

During a snowstorm, catch single snowflakes on a dark piece of paper or fabric and observe them closely. Use a magnifying glass to get a closer look or take a close-up, high-resolution photo with a smartphone or digital camera. What characteristics do you notice about each one?

THE SCIENCE BEHIND THE FUN

Snowflakes have six sides because when water freezes, the molecules arrange themselves in symmetrical hexagonal (six-sided) crystals. Ice is less dense than liquid water because of the space in this structure.

Most commonly, snowflakes form as flat hexagonal shapes called *plates*. If humidity is high, branching occurs and *dendrites* form, growing and spreading to create starlike patterns. Flakes can also form columns or needles depending on the temperature and humidity.

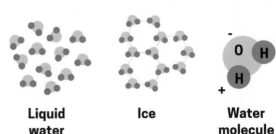

Liquid water   Ice   Water molecule

MAKE A SNOW GLOBE

Make a glitter blizzard inside a recycled jar.

TIME: 30 MINUTES

Fig. 5: Shake the jar to make it snow!

TOOLS & MATERIALS

- clean used jar
- plastic, glass, or metal ornaments or figurines
- hot glue gun and glue sticks
- measuring cup
- clear glue
- warm water
- spoon
- glitter (white, silver, and/or blue)
- measuring spoons

SAFETY TIPS, HINTS & TRICKS

- Choose ornaments and figurines that are least likely to break down or dissolve in water.
- Do this lab near or over a sink or protect your work surface with newspaper or paper towels to absorb any spilled solution.
- Be sure to seal your snow globe very well so nothing leaks out.

PROTOCOL

STEP 1: With the help of an adult, use hot glue to attach your ornaments and figurines to the underside of the jar lid, creating the scene for your globe. Allow the glue to set completely. (Fig. 1)

STEP 2: Add about 2 ounces (60 ml) of clear glue to a jar and add enough water so it's two-thirds full. Use a spoon to thoroughly mix the water and glue.

STEP 3: Add about 2 teaspoons of glitter to the jar and stir it into the water-glue mixture. (Fig. 2)

Fig. 1: Style a winter scene and attach it to the bottom of the lid with hot glue.

Fig. 2: Mix glitter into the water-and-glue solution.

Fig. 3: Test the water level and remove or add water as needed.

Fig. 4: Seal the jar with hot glue applied to the rim.

STEP 4: Place the lid on the jar with the scene facing down into the water-glue-glitter mixture. Add or remove water until the jar is full and there isn't any air inside when the lid is on. (Fig. 3)

STEP 5: Once you determine the final amount of water, remove the lid. Clean and dry the jar's rim, threads, and sides, as well as the lid threads.

STEP 6: Apply a bead of hot glue around the rim and on the threads of the jar. Quickly apply the lid. Make sure it seals tightly. (Fig. 4)

STEP 7: Shake your globe and watch the snow fall on your winter scene! (Fig. 5)

CREATIVE ENRICHMENT: DID YOU KNOW?

When thunder and lightning happen during a snowstorm, it's called "thundersnow." The upward motion of warm, moist air increases snow formation and causes enough electrical charge separation in the clouds for lightning to strike. Thundersnow often coincides with very heavy snow falling at a rate of 1 to 3 inches (5 to 7.5 cm) per hour.

THE SCIENCE BEHIND THE FUN

When you shake your snow globe, you create a tiny blizzard. Real blizzards occur when a mass of warm air collides with a mass of very cold air. The cold air cuts under and the warm air rises upward to form lots of snow. This collision of air masses also creates high-speed winds.

To officially qualify as a blizzard, a snowstorm has to meet the following three criteria:

1. Sustained winds or frequent gusts of 35 miles per hour (56 kph) or greater

2. Considerable amounts of falling, blowing, and drifting snow that reduce visibility to ¼ mile (400 m) or less

3. Prolonged duration—typically 3 hours or more

FAUX SNOW

TOOLS & MATERIALS

- ⊘ disposable diaper(s)
- ⊘ scissors
- ⊘ large glass or plastic dish or other container
- ⊘ measuring cup
- ⊘ water
- ⊘ wintertime animals, trees, and other toys (optional)

Make your own snow equivalent using an unconventional but readily available material.

TIME: 15 MINUTES

Fig. 5: Faux snow is white, wet, fluffy, and cool to the touch. It is also nontoxic and reuseable.

SAFETY TIPS, HINTS & TRICKS

- ⊘ If your "snowflake" particles are too big, ask an adult to help you pulse the wet gel in a blender to reach the desired consistency.

PROTOCOL

STEP 1: Use scissors to cut into the bottom of a disposable diaper. (Fig. 1)

STEP 2: Carefully peel out the white, fluffy stuff that looks like cotton and place it in your dish or container. (Fig. 2)

STEP 3: Add water about a ¼ cup (59 ml) at a time. You can use a measuring cup to see just how much water it will hold. (Hint: It's a lot!) What do you notice? The white stuff should start to moisten and become mushier. (Fig. 3)

Fig. 1: Cut up a diaper.

Fig. 2: Remove the fluffy stuff.

Fig. 3: Gradually moisten the cotton-like material with water.

Fig. 4: Break up the clumps of wet fluff with your fingers.

STEP 4: Use your hands to break up the mixture. It should feel slightly wet and squishy. (Fig. 4)

STEP 5: Place your snow in the fridge for about 15 to 30 minutes to make it colder. After you remove it, add animals, trees, and other toys to create a playful wintertime scene. (Fig. 5).

STEP 6: When you're done with your faux snow, *do not* wash it down the drain or flush it down the toilet—it will clog your pipes! Simply throw it away.

CREATIVE ENRICHMENT: FAUX SNOW #2 MINI LAB

You can make a different kind of fake snow with ¼ cup (60 ml) white hair conditioner and 1½ cups (331 g) baking soda. Mix the two substances together with a spoon or your hands until the mixture clumps enough to form snowballs without crumbling. Add more conditioner or baking soda as needed.

THE SCIENCE BEHIND THE FUN

The fake snow you create using from the diaper contains a common polymer called sodium polyacrylate (pah-li-A-kruh-late), a sodium salt of acrylic acid with the chemical formula $[-CH_2-CH(CO_2Na)-]_n$, where n is the number of units of the salt molecule in the chain.

This material is superabsorbent, with the ability to take on 100 to 1,000 times its weight in water. As fake snow it is nontoxic, feels cool to the touch, lasts for days, and looks similar to the real thing. Unlike real snow, it doesn't melt! And you definitely shouldn't eat it!

Lab 43

FROZEN BUBBLES

Mix water, corn syrup, dish soap, and sugar to make the perfect solution for frozen bubbles.

TIME: 1 HOUR

Fig. 5: When ice crystals appear, your bubble is beginning to freeze!

TOOLS & MATERIALS

- water
- light corn syrup
- dish soap
- white sugar
- bowl
- mixing spoon
- jar
- plastic straw
- metal pan or tray (optional)
- squeezable bottle (optional)
- tape (optional)

SAFETY TIPS, HINTS & TRICKS

- Outdoor temperatures need to be very cold for this experiment to work—about 10°F (−12°C) or colder. Take proper precautions to avoid frostbite.
- The bubble solution can make a sticky, sugary mess if not handled carefully. Be sure to have something nearby for easy cleanup.
- Dish soap should be a regular concentration, not "ultra" or "super."

PROTOCOL

STEP 1: In a bowl, mix together 1 cup (235 ml) warm water and 2 tablespoons (30 ml) each of light corn syrup and dish soap. Add 2 tablespoons (25 g) of granulated white sugar, and stir. (Fig. 1)

STEP 2: Pour the bubble solution into a jar and chill it outside or in the freezer for 30 minutes to lower its temperature. After 30 minutes, stir the solution again. (Fig. 2)

STEP 3: Go outside and find a very cold, textured metal surface to blow your bubbles onto or use a metal pan or tray.

Fig. 1: Mix everything together in a bowl and stir.

Fig. 2: Very cold bubble solution helps the bubbles freeze faster.

Fig. 3: Using a straw to make bubbles instead of a standard bubble wand also reduces the mess.

Fig. 4: Tape a straw to a squeeze bottle and blow bubbles with it.

STEP 4: Instead of using a store-bought wand, blow your bubbles with a straw and your breath. You can be more specific about where you form your bubble. (Fig. 3)

STEP 5: You can rig the straw to a squeeze bottle with a bit of tape and use that to blow bubbles. This keeps your warm breath from interfering with the freezing of the bubble. (Fig. 4)

STEP 6: Even with perfect weather conditions, many of your bubbles will pop before they can freeze. It's good to be patient and to keep trying. When a bubble does freeze, quickly snap a photo of it. Or, even better yet, make a video of the ice crystals forming! (Fig. 5)

CREATIVE ENRICHMENT: KITCHEN FREEZER BUBBLES MINI LAB

Put a small metal sheet pan in the freezer for ten minutes. Pour a bit of very cold bubble solution in the center and use a straw to blow a bubble on it. Once a bubble sticks, gently put the pan back in the freezer. After 5 minutes, check on your bubble. When it appears frosted, carefully remove it from the freezer to take a closer look. If it popped, try again.

THE SCIENCE BEHIND THE FUN

Bubbles are made up of three layers— a thin layer of water sandwiched between two thin layers of soap. When a bubble freezes, it may look like the entire surface is solidifying, but it's really only the innermost layer of water turning to ice within a film of soap.

In the bubble mixture you made, the corn syrup adds thickness, which stabilizes the bubbles, and the sugar provides microscopic seed crystals that speed up the freezing process. These substances also decrease the freezing point of the water, which is why the temperature has to be so cold to get a frozen bubble.

Lab 44

SUPERCOOLED WATER

TOOLS & MATERIALS

- drinking glass
- distilled water
- measuring spoons
- large bowl
- ice
- sea salt
- small dish

SAFETY TIPS, HINTS & TRICKS

- Be sure to use distilled water in this lab. You can find it at the grocery store or drugstore. Mineral water or tap water will not supercool very well because of dissolved impurities.

- Make sure that the glass you use is very clean. Rinse it with distilled water to make extra sure.

Cool water below its freezing point and crystallize it on demand.

TIME: 30 MINUTES

Fig. 3: Supercooled water freezes instantly when it comes into contact with ice.

PROTOCOL

STEP 1: Pour ¼ cup (60 ml) of distilled water into the very clean glass.

STEP 2: Tuck the glass in a large bowl full of ice. (Fig. 1)

STEP 3: Sprinkle 2 tablespoons (36 g) of salt onto the ice, being sure not to get any into the glass of water. (Fig. 2)

STEP 4: Let the glass sit in the ice and salt mixture for 20 to 25 minutes.

STEP 5: Grab a fresh ice cube from the freezer and place it on the small dish. Carefully take the glass out of the bowl of ice and pour the supercooled water over the ice cube. (Fig. 3)

TIP: Agitation, tiny ice crystals, or even specs of dust can all freeze supercooled water before you're able to pour it. If this happens, start over with a clean setup and try the experiment again.

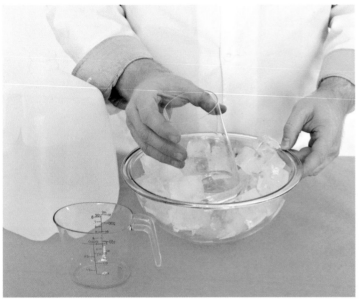

Fig. 1: The level of the ice should be higher than the level of the water.

Fig. 2: Add salt to the ice to begin supercooling.

CREATIVE ENRICHMENT: ICE CREAM IN A BAG MINI LAB

1. Combine 1 cup (5 ml) of half-and-half, 1½ teaspoons (7.5 ml) of vanilla extract, and 1 tablespoon (13 g) of sugar in a 1-quart (946-ml) zip-top bag. Press out any excess air from the bag, seal it firmly, and then seal it in a second bag.

2. Next, fill a 1-gallon (3.8 L) zip-top plastic bag halfway with ice and add ¼ cup (60 g) sea salt. Place the small bag inside the large bag, fill the remaining space with extra ice, and seal it. Protect your hands with gloves or oven mitts and shake the bag for 6 minutes. Take the small bag out and rinse the outside with cold water to get off all the salt. Carefully open the small bag and use a spoon to mix and soften the ice cream. Scoop it out of the bag to enjoy.

THE SCIENCE BEHIND THE FUN

Supercooling is the process of lowering the temperature of a liquid or gas below its freezing point without it becoming a solid. This occurs because of the absence of seed crystals or nuclei around which a crystal structure can form.

Because salt lowers the freezing point of water, it melts ice and converts it into saltwater of the same temperature. While 0°F (−18°C) ice from a freezer will still melt because of salt, its temperature won't increase to 32°F (0°C) like it would with regular melted ice water. Instead, the salt turns it into 0°F (−18°C) water. This creates a salty slurry that is well below freezing and that can supercool water, make ice cream, or quickly chill a drink.

UNIT 7
CLIMATE IN CRISIS

Climate change is real. The Earth is warming, which is raising sea levels, intensifying weather, and damaging ecosystems—and human activity has played a part. While the majority of changes we need to make to control the climate crisis are the responsibility of governments and large corporations, there are things we can do as global citizens to be a part of the solution.

Learn more and teach others about climate change. Use less energy when you can by taking public transportation, walking, or riding a bike. Install energy-efficient light bulbs and appliances in your home and turn them off or unplug them when not in use.

Reduce, reuse, and recycle, and when you buy, buy local, especially food. Eat the food that you do buy so as little of it goes to waste as possible, and eat less meat—industrialized farming releases tons of greenhouse gases into the air. Support sustainable energy sources, such as wind and solar power, because we'll eventually run out of fossil fuels and burning them belches carbon dioxide and pollutants into the atmosphere.

In this unit, you'll start by learning all about global warming and the power of greenhouse gases. You'll turn a T-shirt into a bag and make your own recycled paper, reducing waste and reusing everyday items. You'll also build a simple composting device to turn vegetable scraps into rich soil for plants.

You'll experiment with seed growth under drought and flood conditions and model the melting of the polar ice caps. You'll finish out the unit by building a wind turbine and generating your own electricity. Along the way, be sure to look for opportunities to do your part in the fight against climate change.

CARBON DIOXIDE EXTINGUISHER

TOOLS & MATERIALS

- large glass jar
- measuring spoons
- white vinegar
- matches or lighter
- small candle, such as a votive or tea light
- long, narrow strip of paper
- baking soda
- large bowl or high-sided dish
- soda water

SAFETY TIPS, HINTS & TRICKS

- Your glass jar should be about quart-sized (4 cups [946 ml]).
- This lab uses matches or a lighter to make a flame. Adult supervision is required.

Mix vinegar and baking soda to create and learn all about the properties of a greenhouse gas.

TIME: 20 MINUTES

Fig. 4: Pour the carbon dioxide down the chute and onto the candle flame.

PROTOCOL

STEP 1: Pour 5 tablespoons (75 ml) of white vinegar into the jar. (Fig. 1)

STEP 2: Have an adult use the matches or lighter to light the candle wick. Meanwhile, fold a strip of paper in half lengthwise to create a chute. (Fig. 2)

STEP 3: Add ½ tablespoon (7 g) of baking soda to the vinegar. The mixture should bubble and fizz rapidly as a chemical reaction occurs and releases carbon dioxide gas. (Fig. 3)

Fig. 1: Add vinegar to a quart-sized jar.

Fig. 2: Carefully light the candle and fold a paper chute.

Fig. 3: Mix the baking soda and vinegar to cause a reaction.

Fig. 5: Light a candle in the bottom of a bowl. Pour soda water in the bowl around the candle.

STEP 4: Quickly but carefully pour the gas down the paper chute toward the candle. Be sure not to pour out any vinegar or baking soda. What do you observe? (Fig. 4)

STEP 5: Try an alternative version of the same experiment: Place your candle in the bottom of the bowl or dish and have your adult light it.

STEP 6: Carefully pour soda water (which contains dissolved carbon dioxide) around it, being sure not to get any on the wick. What do you observe? (Fig. 5)

CREATIVE ENRICHMENT: FROZEN CO$_2$ MINI LAB

Have an adult get some frozen carbon dioxide, known as "dry ice." Use caution and wear protective goggles and gloves when handling it. Fill a tall jar or glass halfway with water. Add a single chunk of dry ice. What happens? Add about 1 teaspoon (5 ml) of dish soap to the water. What happens now?

THE SCIENCE BEHIND THE FUN

A flame requires oxygen to keep burning. If the oxygen is cut off or replaced with something else, the flame will go out. Carbon dioxide is heavier than air, so when you pour it out of the glass, it travels down the chute right to the candle, and it stays at the surface of the soda water you pour into the bowl. In both cases, it displaces oxygen and extinguishes the flame.

Carbon dioxide is an important part of our atmosphere because it is very good at holding heat from the sun against the surface of the planet. But when there is too much of it, it traps too much heat and contributes to global warming.

BUILD A TERRARIUM

Plant a small garden in a glass container to learn about the greenhouse effect.

TIME: 45 MINUTES

Fig. 5: A finished terrarium with succulents.

TOOLS & MATERIALS

- ⊘ clear glass container, preferably with a lid
- ⊘ pebbles or small stones
- ⊘ activated charcoal
- ⊘ potting soil
- ⊘ small plants and moss of different colors and shapes
- ⊘ water
- ⊘ spray bottle (optional)
- ⊘ decorative elements, such as rocks, crystals, and shells (optional)

SAFETY TIPS, HINTS & TRICKS

- ⊘ Be sure your glass container is thoroughly clean.
- ⊘ Small plants, such as succulents, won't grow too quickly or get too big for the container.
- ⊘ A spray bottle with water is a good way to hydrate your plants while preventing overwatering.

PROTOCOL

STEP 1: Add a 1-inch (2.5 cm) layer of stones to the bottom of your container. (Fig. 1)

STEP 2: Add a ½-inch (1 cm) layer of activated charcoal on top of the stones. (Fig. 2)

STEP 3: Fill the container halfway with potting soil. (Fig. 3)

STEP 4: Plant your plants and moss. Carefully separate the roots to remove some of the soil they came in. Leave space for them to grow. Pat down the soil so they stay in place. (Fig. 4)

Fig. 1: A layer of rocks helps with drainage and prevents root rot.

Fig. 2: Charcoal filters water and prevents mold and mildew.

Fig. 3: Finish building the ground of the terrarium with a layer of potting soil.

Fig. 4: Space out your plants so they have room to grow.

STEP 5: Water your plants and place your container in indirect light. Add decorative elements, if you're using them, and put the lid on if there is one.

STEP 6: Observe your terrarium over the course of the next few days, weeks, and months. What do you notice about the growth of the plants and environment inside the container? (Fig. 5)

TIP: If you start to see too much condensation inside your closed terrarium, take off the lid once every few days to dry it out a bit.

CREATIVE ENRICHMENT: GREENHOUSE EFFECT MINI LAB

Pour 2 cups (475 ml) of cold water into each of two identical glass jars. Add an equal number of cubes to each and stir. Take and record the temperature of each jar, then enclose one jar in a clear plastic bag. Place both jars in the sun. After an hour, measure the temperature again. What do you notice? How does this setup demonstrate the greenhouse effect?

THE SCIENCE BEHIND THE FUN

The air inside a greenhouse (or terrarium) can become quite warm. The structure's glass walls let in the sun's rays and light energy warms the air, soil, and plants. The glass holds in this heat, creating a mini climate.

Over the past few centuries, carbon dioxide and methane created by human activities have built up in the atmosphere. In high concentrations, these gases act like greenhouse glass, holding in heat from the sun.

The result is that the Earth is getting warmer. This means a rise in global air and ocean temperatures, which could lead to stronger weather systems, melting polar ice and rising sea levels, and the collapse of certain ecosystems.

UPCYCLED T-SHIRT BAG

Turn an old T-shirt into a reusable tote bag.

TIME: 45 MINUTES

Fig. 5: Take your bag everywhere and never use plastic again!

TOOLS & MATERIALS

- T-shirt
- scissors
- strong twine, string, or yarn
- large safety pin
- fabric markers or fabric paint (optional)
- piece of thick cardboard (if using markers or paint)

SAFETY TIPS, HINTS & TRICKS

- Instead of decorating a plain shirt, you can use a T-shirt with a logo or other image that you like already on it.
- Sharp scissors for cutting fabric work best for this lab. Have an adult help.
- When you pull sideways on the cut edges of T-shirt material, it curls inward, giving your bag a cleaner look.
- Place a piece of thick cardboard between the layers of your T-shirt to keep paint and markers from bleeding through to the other side.

PROTOCOL

STEP 1: Lay your shirt flat. Use the scissors to cut off the sleeves. Cut 1 or 2 inches (2.5 or 5 cm) beyond the seam where the sleeve connects to the body of the shirt. Make these handle holes large enough to fit over your shoulder.

STEP 2: Make a round cut a few inches (7.5 cm) from the collar seam, removing the neck of the shirt, to form the inside of the handles and the top edge of the bag. (Fig. 1)

STEP 3: If you're decorating the bag, pull the cut T-shirt over the piece of cardboard. Use your fabric markers or

Fig. 1: Cut out the neck to make the T-shirt look more like a tank top.

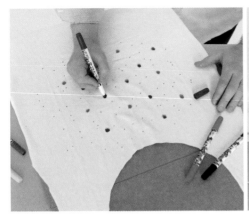

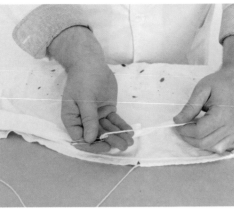

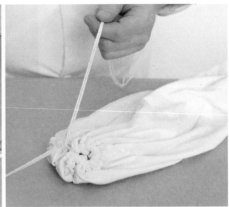

Fig. 2: Insert a piece of thick cardboard and embellish both sides of the shirt.

Fig. 3: Run the safety pin around the inside of the hem, pulling the string with it to make a drawstring.

Fig. 4: Gather the tails and tie off the bottom of the bag.

paint to decorate the outside of your bag. Let one side dry completely before decorating the other. (Fig. 2)

STEP 4: Cut two small slits in the bottom hem of the T-shirt: one centered on the front and one centered on the back.

STEP 5: Tie a length of string or yarn around the end of the safety pin and insert it into one of the slits. Use your fingers and the pin to work the string through the hem, around to the other slit. (Fig. 3)

STEP 6: Pull the string to gather the hem, closing up half of the bottom of the bag.

STEP 7: Repeat Steps 5 and 6 for the other side of the hem. Tie all the ends of string together in a secure knot, completely closing off the hole in the bag's bottom, and trim the tails. (Fig. 4)

STEP 8: Take your bag to the beach to carry your towel, sunscreen, and a great book or to the grocery store to carry your food! (Fig. 5)

CREATIVE ENRICHMENT: TAKING IT FURTHER

- What other pieces of clothing can you "upcycle" (with permission first!) into something new and useful?

- Instead of a store-bought costume for your next Halloween or theme party, what can you come up with using materials you already have?

THE SCIENCE BEHIND THE FUN

One of the best ways you can benefit the planet is by making sure at least 50 percent of your clothes come from secondhand sources, such as thrift, vintage, and consignment stores.

The global, seasonal, "fast fashion" industry puts great stress on the environment, polluting millions of gallons of water through making and dyeing fabric and increasing carbon emissions by constantly transporting materials, goods, and waste around the world.

Secondhand fashion keeps tons of clothes out of landfills, where they take hundreds of years to break down and release heavy metals into the soil and methane into the air.

Lab 48

MAKE RECYCLED PAPER

Use a blender, newspaper, and water to make your very own paper from recycled materials.

TIME: 1 DAY

Fig. 6: Use your recycled paper as you would any other piece of paper.

TOOLS & MATERIALS

- ◇ old picture frame, 5" × 7" or 8" × 10" (13 × 18 cm or 20 × 25 cm)
- ◇ piece of screen or mesh
- ◇ heavy-duty scissors
- ◇ hot glue gun and hot glue sticks
- ◇ large container or kitchen sink
- ◇ water
- ◇ 4 full sheets of newspaper
- ◇ blender
- ◇ large measuring cup
- ◇ school glue
- ◇ measuring spoons
- ◇ mixing spoon
- ◇ craft knife

SAFETY TIPS, HINTS & TRICKS

- ◇ This lab uses tools and appliances that require adult assistance and supervision.
- ◇ Be sure to use paper that is not coated or glossy in any way. Newspaper and used notebook or printer paper work for this lab, but avoid using magazine pages.
- ◇ You can make an alternative papermaking frame by stretching pantyhose over a wire hanger bent into a rectangle.

Fig. 1: Construct a papermaking tool using an old frame and some screen or mesh.

Fig. 2: Add the blended paper slurry to the container or sink of water.

Fig. 3: Slowly draw the frame up through the mixture of water, paper, and glue, catching paper fibers on the screen.

PROTOCOL

STEP 1: If your picture frame has glass and/or a backing, remove them and set them aside. With heavy-duty scissors, trim a piece of screen or mesh to fit across the opening of the frame. Secure it in place with hot glue. (Fig. 1)

STEP 2: Fill your container or sink with at least 4 inches (10 cm) of water. While the sink is filling, tear your paper into 2-inch (5 cm) squares.

STEP 3: Ask an adult to help you blend 4 cups (950 ml) of water with half of the torn-up paper. Add additional water if needed, until all the paper has broken down completely. Do this a second time with the remaining half of torn-up paper.

STEP 4: Pour both batches of the slurry into the container or sink of water, add 4 tablespoons (60 ml) of school glue, and stir thoroughly until the glue is completely dissolved. (Fig. 2)

STEP 5: Scoop your papermaking frame to the bottom of the container or sink and lift it up through the slurry very slowly, counting to 20 as you go. (Fig. 3)

CONTINUED

**CREATIVE ENRICHMENT:
TAKING IT FURTHER**

1. Add other recycled elements to your slurry, such as small scraps of fabric, bits of thread, or even dryer lint. Use a natural dye, such as turmeric or cabbage juice, to color your paper.

2. Add dried flower petals and seeds to the paper pulp when it is still wet on the screen. If you bury the dried paper under a thin layer of soil, the seeds will sprout and grow.

Fig. 4: Drain as much water as possible.

Fig. 5: Make sure your paper is completely dry before you peel it off the frame.

STEP 6: Once you have lifted the frame out of the slurry, let it drain for about a minute. (Fig. 4)

STEP 7: Let the paper dry directly on the screen for a day or two. Like in Lab 16 (page 52), you can speed up the drying process with an electric fan or hair dryer.

STEP 8: Once the paper is completely dry, carefully peel it off the frame. If necessary, use a craft knife to carefully cut around the edges to release the paper. (Fig. 5)

STEP 9: Use your paper to write a letter to a friend or make a recycled paper craft. Fold it into a card or make a bunch of pieces and put them together as a small book. (Fig. 6)

THE SCIENCE BEHIND THE FUN

In the real world, paper to be recycled is collected, sorted, and shredded. Water and chemicals are added to break down the fibers into an oatmeal-like slurry called *pulp*, which is passed through screens and spinners and flotation tanks to remove impurities. The fibers are bleached and then passed through vibrating machines and over rollers that remove excess water. The paper is pressed into large, flat sheets that are gathered on rolls before being cut and packaged.

Recycling paper saves trees, oil, landfill space, energy, and water. And, the trees that aren't cut down go on to absorb carbon dioxide for years. The only limit to recycling is that paper fibers are shortened each time they're processed and can only be recycled five to seven times before it is best to just compost them.

COMPOSTING IN ACTION

Reduce the amount of waste you produce and make useful soil by harnessing the power of composting.

TIME: 1 MONTH (AT LEAST)

Fig. 6: The compost is ready to use when it is brown and crumbly and smells earthy, like soil.

TOOLS & MATERIALS

- 2-liter soda bottle
- utility or craft knife
- masking or painter's tape
- soil
- water
- spray bottle
- fruit or vegetable scraps
- granulated garden fertilizer
- measuring spoons
- dry leaves or other plant material
- other compostable materials
- thermometer

SAFETY TIPS, HINTS & TRICKS

- Composting takes time, and you might not get final results from this lab for at least a month. Patience is the key here.
- In addition to the items listed under Tools & Materials, compostable materials include plant debris from the garden and household waste, such as shredded newspaper, tea bags, coffee grounds, and eggshells.
- Do not use meat, fat, dairy products, or pet/animal waste in your composter.

CONTINUED

Fig. 1: Cut the bottle so it has a flip top.

Fig. 2: Moistened soil introduces microorganisms to the compost container.

Fig. 3: Layer scraps and other materials in the bottle.

PROTOCOL

STEP 1: Rinse out the bottle, remove the label, and screw the cap on firmly. Make a flip top in the bottle by cutting it with the knife (and the help of an adult) most of the way around, about a quarter of the way down the bottle. (Fig. 1)

STEP 2: Place a layer of soil in the bottom of the bottle. Moisten the soil with water from the spray bottle if it is dry. (Fig. 2)

STEP 3: Add a thin layer of fruit or vegetable scraps, another thin layer of soil, 1 tablespoon (15 g) of fertilizer, and a layer of dry leaves. Continue adding layers of compostable materials until the bottle is almost full. (Fig. 3)

STEP 4: Tape the top of the bottle in place and put it in a sunny location. (Fig. 4)

STEP 5: Roll the bottle around every day to mix the contents. If moisture condenses inside the bottle, open the cap periodically to let it dry out a little. If the contents look too dry, add a squirt or two of water from the spray bottle. What do you notice as the days pass? What kinds of smells come from your compost? (Fig. 5)

STEP 6: After a week or so, use a thermometer to take the temperature of the contents of the compost container. How does it compare with the air temperature? How does compost make its own heat?

STEP 7: It takes about a month for the compost to become crumbly and entirely brown, making it ready to use for planting. How does the compost affect the growth of what's planted in it? (Fig. 6)

Fig. 4: Tape the bottle closed.

Fig. 5: Mixing the contents speeds up the rate of composting.

CREATIVE ENRICHMENT: WORM COMPOSTING MINI LAB

1. To make a "worm farm," poke or drill several small holes in the top, sides, and bottom of a 1-foot (61 cm) square plastic bin. Add 6 inches (15 cm) of torn newspaper strips. Mist this bedding with water until it is saturated, then add a thin layer of soil. Add 1 pound (450 g) of red wiggler worms (*Eisenia fetida*).

2. Feed the worms by tucking fruit and vegetable scraps and other compostable materials into the bedding. Avoid animal products and citrus. Start with two handfuls of scraps twice a week and reduce or increase the amount of food as needed.

THE SCIENCE BEHIND THE FUN

During composting, microorganisms in the soil eat organic waste and break it down into its simplest parts. This requires oxygen (which mixes in from the air when you turn the container) and produces heat.

Organic materials in landfills generate methane gas. But when enough people compost food waste and other materials, we use less landfill space and greatly reduce emissions. In agriculture, compost can be incredibly beneficial, eliminating the need for synthetic chemical fertilizers and promoting higher yields of crops.

DROUGHTS & FLOODS EXPERIMENT

TOOLS & MATERIALS

- ⊙ 80 mung bean seeds
- ⊙ 4 medium plastic containers
- ⊙ paper towels
- ⊙ plastic wrap
- ⊙ pushpin or straight pin
- ⊙ aluminum foil
- ⊙ water
- ⊙ spray bottle
- ⊙ masking tape
- ⊙ marker

SAFETY TIPS, HINTS & TRICKS

- ⊙ If you can't find mung bean seeds, seeds such as peas and beans can be used instead. You need something that sprouts quickly.
- ⊙ The best plastic containers to use are 16-ounce (475 ml) deli containers or large yogurt or cream cheese tubs.

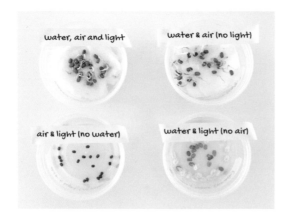

Sprout mung bean seeds under different conditions to demonstrate the effects of climate change on growing food.

TIME: 7 TO 10 DAYS

Fig. 5: All four tubs after a week of germination and growth

PROTOCOL

STEP 1: Soak all the mung bean seeds in water for a couple of hours. This will speed up germination.

STEP 2: Put twenty seeds into a container on their own. Make a label with a marker and a piece of tape that tells you what elements are being tested. In this case, the label should read "air & light (no water)." (Fig. 1)

STEP 3: Set up a second container with twenty seeds and add water until the seeds are completely submerged. Label this tub "water & light (no air)." (Fig. 2)

Fig. 1: Tub #1 with just seeds

Fig. 2: Tub #2 with submerged seeds

Fig. 3: Tub #3 with a moist paper towel surface for the seeds and a perforated plastic wrap cover

Fig. 4: Tub #4 is kept in the dark by wrapping it in foil.

STEP 4: Set up a third container with a moist, flat surface inside made from wet paper towels. Place twenty seeds on the paper towel, seal the tub with plastic wrap, and poke a few small holes in the top with the pin. Label this tub "water, air & light." (Fig. 3)

STEP 5: Set up the final container the same as Step 4 except instead of plastic wrap, wrap the entire container in foil to keep the light out. Leave an overhang flap on one side to let air in but still keep light out. Label this tub "water & air (no light)." (Fig. 4)

STEP 6: Place all the tubs in a bright, warm spot and check on them every day, making sure the moist environments stay moist. For the submerged seeds, change the water daily to prevent other organisms from growing.

STEP 7: After 7 to 10 days, examine the contents of each tub. A mung bean root is white. The green shoot may have leaves on it. Which conditions led to the best growth? (Fig. 5)

CREATIVE ENRICHMENT: TAKING IT FURTHER

1. How do cold or hot temperatures affect sprouting and growth? What if the seeds are damaged with cuts or punctures (as from pests)?

2. Can you use a light bulb instead of sunlight to sprout seeds? How do different wavelengths of light affect the seeds?

THE SCIENCE BEHIND THE FUN

The amount of water in a region can decrease because of the weather but also because of human over-consumption, engineering projects such as dams, or water pollution. Drought affects our lives in many ways because water is an important part of so much human activity. We need it to live and to grow, process, and prepare our food.

Not enough water is a bad thing, but so is too much water. Seeds that are constantly submerged do not sprout well. Flooding also washes away topsoil, giving seeds nothing in which to root. And while a container with air and water but no light does the best in terms of germination, plants eventually need all the elements to keep growing.

MELTING ICE CAPS

TOOLS & MATERIALS

- ⟩ two 6- to 7-inch (15- to 18-cm) diameter bowls
- ⟩ water
- ⟩ blue food coloring
- ⟩ freezer
- ⟩ large, low container, such as a metal tray or plastic bin
- ⟩ stones
- ⟩ toys and shells to represent animals, buildings, and people
- ⟩ ruler
- ⟩ timer

SAFETY TIPS, HINTS & TRICKS

- ⟩ Get help from an adult when freezing water to make your ice caps.
- ⟩ Wear protective gloves when handling the food coloring and the ice to keep from dyeing your hands.

Freeze your own ice caps and model how sea levels rise when they melt.

TIME: 1 DAY

Fig. 5: The water level rises as the ice melts, and the water flows from the land to the sea.

PROTOCOL

STEP 1: Fill both bowls with water and add 5 drops of food coloring to each to tint the water blue. Place the bowls in a freezer until the water is solid. (Fig. 1)

STEP 2: In the low container, arrange the stones in two large piles to represent land masses.

STEP 3: Add ½ to 1 inch (1.3 to 2.5 cm) of water to the container. Measure with a ruler to get an exact depth. Note the water level of the land masses. (Fig. 2)

Fig. 1: Freeze two domes of blue ice.

Fig. 2: Build landmasses out of piles of stones and add water to the container to act as the ocean.

Fig. 3: Place the domes of ice on the landmasses.

Fig. 4: Populate the coasts of your landmasses with animals, structures, and people.

STEP 4: Remove the ice from the bowls and place each piece flat side down on a landmass to act as an ice cap. (Fig. 3)

STEP 5: Add toys and shells along the "coasts" of each of your stone landmasses. (Fig. 4)

STEP 6: Measure the water level with the ruler every 30 minutes to an hour. What do you observe as the ice continues to melt? (Fig. 5)

STEP 7: Once the domes of ice have completely melted, take a final measurement of the water level. How has the encroaching water affected the toys and figures?

CREATIVE ENRICHMENT: SEA ICE MINI LAB

Start with the container full of water and float the blue ice domes in it like icebergs. Measure the depth of the water. Over time, as this "sea ice" melts, is there a change in the water level? Why or why not? What is the difference between melting land ice and melting sea ice?

THE SCIENCE BEHIND THE FUN

At the North and South Poles, snow falls, melts, and falls again. Each new layer of precipitation makes the snowpack harder and more compressed. Over time the lower layers become so compacted that a huge mass of solid ice forms—an ice cap, a glacier, or an ice sheet.

These vast spans of ice have a great impact on the global climate. When they melt, all the fresh water that they hold returns to the oceans, where it can change currents, affect conditions for wildlife, and raise global sea levels. More water means more absorbed heat from sunlight that normally would have been reflected back into space by white ice, which speeds up the melting process.

BUILD A WIND TURBINE

TOOLS & MATERIALS

- small hobby motor (6 to 12 volts)
- low voltage (2.0 to 2.2 volts) LED
- 4 thin craft sticks
- hot glue gun and hot glue sticks
- small paper or plastic cup, about 3 ounces (89 ml)
- scissors
- medium paper or plastic cup, about 9 ounces (266 ml)
- awl or small drill
- strong fan or hair dryer

SAFETY TIPS, HINTS & TRICKS

- This lab involves some simple electrical parts that require the assistance of an adult.
- Also, have an adult poke or drill the hole in the center of the craft stick windmill.

Install a small motor and an LED in a homemade windmill to learn about wind energy.

TIME: 1 HOUR

Fig. 6: Make the windmill spin to generate electricity that lights the LED.

PROTOCOL

STEP 1: Create the curved blades of your turbine by cutting the sides of a small paper cup into four equal parts and then cutting out the bottom. (Fig. 1)

STEP 2: Use hot glue to attach two craft sticks together so they're perpendicular. Once the glue sets, have an adult use the awl or drill to make a small hole in the center that is the same diameter as the motor shaft. (Fig. 2)

STEP 3: Use hot glue to attach the edge of a blade to each end of the craft sticks. Tend them to one side in an off-center position so they catch the wind. (Fig. 3)

Fig. 1: Cut four blades for the windmill out of a small cup.

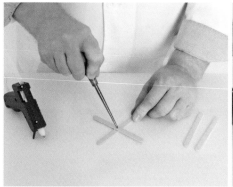

Fig. 2: Connect the craft sticks with hot glue and poke or drill a hole at their intersection.

Fig. 3: Hot glue the blades to the craft stick ends to make a windmill.

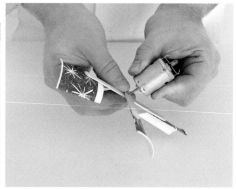

Fig. 4: Attach the blade frame to the front and the LED to the back of the motor.

STEP 4: Attach the LED to the back of the motor by bending each leg of it through a different terminal, and slide your windmill onto the shaft of the motor. (Fig. 4)

STEP 5: Hot-glue the remaining two craft sticks on either side of the larger cup. Glue the other ends to either side of the motor. (Fig. 5)

STEP 6: Test out your turbine with a strong fan or a hair dryer. Does your turbine light the LED? (Fig. 6)

TIP: The LED only works in one direction in a DC circuit. If it doesn't light up, try switching the legs and leads, or reverse the direction of the windmill.

Fig. 5: Build a stand and make sure the blades turn freely.

THE SCIENCE BEHIND THE FUN

Wind turbines use the power of the wind to make electricity. Wind turns the propeller-like blades around a rotor, which spins a generator. This generator doesn't actually create the electricity—it converts mechanical energy into electrical energy.

In this lab, the hobby motor is used in reverse, producing electricity by being moved rather than moving by consuming electricity. The blades capture the wind and move the rotor, which transfers mechanical energy to the motor, so it works like a generator. The lit LED shows that current is flowing.

CREATIVE ENRICHMENT: TAKING IT FURTHER

Make a bunch of different blade frames with different materials that you can swap on and off the motor shaft. What do you observe with each design you test? Which makes best use of the wind?

RESOURCES & REFERENCES

American Kitefliers Association
www.kite.org

American Meteor Society
www.amsmeteors.org

American Meteorological Society
www.ametsoc.org

Fridays for Future
fridaysforfuture.org

National Aeronautics and Space Administration (NASA)
www.nasa.gov

NASA Climate Kids
www.climatekids.nasa.gov

NASA Global Climate Change: Vital Signs of the Planet
climate.nasa.gov

National Geographic Society
www.nationalgeographic.com

National Geographic Kids
www.kids.nationalgeographic.com

National Hurricane Center
www.nhc.noaa.gov

National Oceanic and Atmospheric Administration
www.noaa.gov

National Weather Service
www.weather.gov

Relative Humidity Calculators
www.ringbell.co.uk/info/humid.htm

Royal Meteorological Society
www.rmets.org

Smithsonian National Air and Space Museum
www.airandspace.si.edu

Uncle Jim's Worm Farm
www.unclejimswormfarm.com

United Nations Environment Programme
www.unep.org

United States Environmental Protection Agency
www.epa.gov

ACKNOWLEDGMENTS

Without my dear family and friends, this book would not have been possible. Thank you especially to the following people:

My amazing husband, Joshua, who since day one has been my rock and cheerleader on this project, giving me invaluable feedback and advice with love and patience.

The fabulous Dr. Kenne Dibner, who gave me the confidence that I could write a science book for kids and pointed me in the right direction with sound research and amazing resources.

The incomparable Martha Stewart, her assistant Heather, and my amazing TV crafts teacher-sisters, Hosanna, Kir, and Kristin, whose continued support and encouragement have been integral to Professor Figgy's success.

Our exceptional photographer Christina Bohn, who opened her lovely home to a whirlwind of weather experiments, and whose humor and generosity of spirit were a delight. And the amazing Rob Tannenbaum, who so generously shared his excellent photos of Martha Stewart and Professor Figgy on set together.

Jonathan Simcosky, Meredith Quinn, Anne Re, Hannah Moushabeck, and the entire team at Quarry Books, whose guidance, patience, enthusiasm, and encouragement have made this such an amazing learning process.

My equally weather-obsessed brother, Ryan, my childhood partner-in-crime, who always agreed to watch the Weather Channel and pored over the "Local Forecast" with me day and night looking for hurricanes and nor'easters.

And finally, my parents, Jane and Jim Sr., who have always understood the value of creativity and learning, giving me building blocks and chemistry sets early on, encouraging me with love and support to get out and explore the world, and teaching me that I could grow up to be whoever and whatever I wanted to be.

ABOUT THE AUTHOR

Jim Noonan was born in Newport News, Virginia, and grew up in Westerly, Rhode Island. As a tried-and-true New Englander fond of the region's four seasons, he had a front-row seat to some of the most incredible and striking weather in the world. Raised on Mr. Rogers and Mr. Wizard, with a healthy dose of building blocks and chemistry sets, he developed a passion for creativity, science, and learning at a very young age.

Jim graduated from Dartmouth College, where he studied theater and was pre-med, and received an MFA in acting from the Yale School of Drama, where he was artistic director of the Yale Cabaret in his third year. He moved to New York City to pursue acting professionally and started a small theater company called Fabulous Productions, producing and performing original work for almost a decade.

While working as a crafter in the art department at *The Martha Stewart Show*, Jim brought his dual loves of science and crafting to on-air appearances with Martha herself, sharing the wonders of kitchen science and crystal growing with audiences across the globe. Along the way he developed Professor Figgy's Fabulous Science Kits (www.professorfiggy.com), a popular line of educational, science-based crafting kits for kids, families, and teachers.

After more than fifteen years of working in New York City as a creative professional for clients such as Ralph Lauren Home, Martha Stewart Crafts, ABC's *The Chew*, and Scholastic's *Instructor Magazine*, Jim started a creative projects business of his very own. Most recently, he opened an online lifestyle shop called Bergen Street, where he makes and sells bespoke textiles and vintage home decor.

Jim lives in the Flatbush neighborhood of Brooklyn with his husband, who is an attorney. When he's not hard at work formulating fabulous science kits or sewing up a storm, he likes to get away with friends and family to the Catskill Mountains in upstate New York or travel elsewhere in the world. Iceland is one of his favorite countries, with its stunning combination of gorgeous scenery and fascinating Earth science, and he can't wait to get back there very soon!

INDEX